OPPOSING
VIEWPOINTS®
SERIES

Agricultural Subsidies

Other Books of Related Interest:

Opposing Viewpoints Series

Malnutrition

At Issue Series

Genetically Modified Food

Current Controversies Series

The Global Food Crisis

"Congress shall make no law . . . abridging the freedom of speech, or of the press."

First Amendment to the U.S. Constitution

The basic foundation of our democracy is the First Amendment guarantee of freedom of expression. The Opposing Viewpoints Series is dedicated to the concept of this basic freedom and the idea that it is more important to practice it than to enshrine it.

Agricultural Subsidies

Noël Merino, Book Editor

GREENHAVEN PRESS
A part of Gale, Cengage Learning

GALE
CENGAGE Learning™

Detroit • New York • San Francisco • New Haven, Conn • Waterville, Maine • London

Christine Nasso, *Publisher*
Elizabeth Des Chenes, *Managing Editor*

© 2010 Greenhaven Press, a part of Gale, Cengage Learning.

Gale and Greenhaven Press are registered trademarks used herein under license.

For more information, contact:
Greenhaven Press
27500 Drake Rd.
Farmington Hills, MI 48331-3535
Or you can visit our Internet site at gale.cengage.com

For product information and technology assistance, contact us at

Gale Customer Support, 1-800-877-4253
For permission to use material from this text or product, submit all requests online at www.cengage.com/permissions

Further permissions questions can be emailed to permissionrequest@cengage.com

Articles in Greenhaven Press anthologies are often edited for length to meet page requirements. In addition, original titles of these works are changed to clearly present the main thesis and to explicitly indicate the author's opinion. Every effort is made to ensure that Greenhaven Press accurately reflects the original intent of the authors. Every effort has been made to trace the owners of copyrighted material.

Cover Image copyright Sima, 2009. Used under license from Shutterstock.com.

LIBRARY OF CONGRESS CATALOGING-IN-PUBLICATION DATA

Agricultural subsidies / Noël Merino, book editor.
    p. cm. -- (Opposing viewpoints)
    Includes bibliographical references and index.
    ISBN 978-0-7377-4500-9 (hardcover)
    ISBN 978-0-7377-4501-6 (pbk.)
    1. Agricultural subsidies. 2. Agriculture and state. I. Merino, Noël. II. Series: Opposing viewpoints series (Unnumbered)
    HD1415.A3223 2009
    338.1'8--dc22

                                                    2009018937

Printed in the United States of America
1 2 3 4 5 6 7 13 12 11 10 09

Contents

Chapter 3: Should Agricultural Subsidies Be Eliminated?

Chapter 4: What Are Some Alternatives to Agricultural Subsidies?

Why Consider Opposing Viewpoints?

> *"The only way in which a human being can make some approach to knowing the whole of a subject is by hearing what can be said about it by persons of every variety of opinion and studying all modes in which it can be looked at by every character of mind. No wise man ever acquired his wisdom in any mode but this."*
>
> John Stuart Mill

In our media-intensive culture it is not difficult to find differing opinions. Thousands of newspapers and magazines and dozens of radio and television talk shows resound with differing points of view. The difficulty lies in deciding which opinion to agree with and which "experts" seem the most credible. The more inundated we become with differing opinions and claims, the more essential it is to hone critical reading and thinking skills to evaluate these ideas. Opposing Viewpoints books address this problem directly by presenting stimulating debates that can be used to enhance and teach these skills. The varied opinions contained in each book examine many different aspects of a single issue. While examining these conveniently edited opposing views, readers can develop critical thinking skills such as the ability to compare and contrast authors' credibility, facts, argumentation styles, use of persuasive techniques, and other stylistic tools. In short, the Opposing Viewpoints Series is an ideal way to attain the higher-level thinking and reading skills so essential in a culture of diverse and contradictory opinions.

In addition to providing a tool for critical thinking, Opposing Viewpoints books challenge readers to question their own strongly held opinions and assumptions. Most people form their opinions on the basis of upbringing, peer pressure, and personal, cultural, or professional bias. By reading carefully balanced opposing views, readers must directly confront new ideas as well as the opinions of those with whom they disagree. This is not to simplistically argue that everyone who reads opposing views will—or should—change his or her opinion. Instead, the series enhances readers' understanding of their own views by encouraging confrontation with opposing ideas. Careful examination of others' views can lead to the readers' understanding of the logical inconsistencies in their own opinions, perspective on why they hold an opinion, and the consideration of the possibility that their opinion requires further evaluation.

Evaluating Other Opinions

To ensure that this type of examination occurs, Opposing Viewpoints books present all types of opinions. Prominent spokespeople on different sides of each issue as well as well-known professionals from many disciplines challenge the reader. An additional goal of the series is to provide a forum for other, less known, or even unpopular viewpoints. The opinion of an ordinary person who has had to make the decision to cut off life support from a terminally ill relative, for example, may be just as valuable and provide just as much insight as a medical ethicist's professional opinion. The editors have two additional purposes in including these less known views. One, the editors encourage readers to respect others' opinions—even when not enhanced by professional credibility. It is only by reading or listening to and objectively evaluating others' ideas that one can determine whether they are worthy of consideration. Two, the inclusion of such viewpoints encourages the important critical thinking skill of objectively evaluating an author's credentials and bias. This evaluation will illuminate an author's reasons for taking a particular stance on an issue and will aid in readers' evaluation of the author's ideas.

It is our hope that these books will give readers a deeper understanding of the issues debated and an appreciation of the complexity of even seemingly simple issues when good and honest people disagree. This awareness is particularly important in a democratic society such as ours in which people enter into public debate to determine the common good. Those with whom one disagrees should not be regarded as enemies but rather as people whose views deserve careful examination and may shed light on one's own.

Thomas Jefferson once said that "difference of opinion leads to inquiry, and inquiry to truth." Jefferson, a broadly educated man, argued that "if a nation expects to be ignorant and free . . . it expects what never was and never will be." As individuals and as a nation, it is imperative that we consider the opinions of others and examine them with skill and discernment. The Opposing Viewpoints Series is intended to help readers achieve this goal.

David L. Bender and Bruno Leone,
Founders

Introduction

> "U.S. prominence in global markets coupled with large U.S. subsidy levels have directed much international attention to U.S. cotton program outlays in recent years."
>
> —Randy Schnepf,
> Specialist in Agricultural Policy,
> Resources, Science, and Industry Division,
> USDA Economic Research Service

According to the U.S. Department of Agriculture (USDA), the top three producers of cotton—China, the United States, and India—together produce over half the world's cotton. Although China produces the most cotton in the world, the United States is the leading exporter of cotton, with its trade accounting for over one-third of the global trade in raw cotton. African countries, including Burkina Faso, Benin, Mali, Zimbabwe, Egypt, Tanzania, Cameroon, Côte d'Ivoire, Nigeria, Sudan, Chad, Zambia, Malawi, Mozambique, and Senegal, together account for a significant portion of the export trade in raw cotton. All these countries compete globally for a share of the world cotton export market, and garnering a bigger share of that market depends upon offering a competitive price for cotton. The agricultural subsidies that the United States provides cotton farmers has been an issue of great contention recently, as other countries claim that such subsidies distort trade and negatively affect their livelihood by allowing U.S. farmers to unfairly offer lower prices for their cotton exports.

According to a 2004 report by the Food and Agriculture Organization of the United Nations (FAO), the effects of cotton subsidies in the United States are significant for cotton farmers in the developing world. In particular, the West African nations of Mali, Burkina Faso, Chad, and Benin rely on cotton revenue for the bulk of their national income. Whereas cotton production costs in West Africa are very low, in the United States costs are three times as high. Nonetheless, since U.S. cotton farmers receive billions of dollars in subsidies and support, U.S. cotton farmers are able to price their cotton lower than African farmers.

Oxfam released a study in 2007 that argued for the reform of American cotton subsidies. Oxfam claims that between two and three million farms in West Africa rely on cotton as their main source of income. Because they have to compete with farms in the United States for a share of the world export market, any subsidies given to American farmers make it harder for African farmers to compete in the export market. For West African countries that depend heavily on the income from cotton, Oxfam estimates that eliminating U.S. cotton subsidies would result in income increased by 8 to 20 percent. Because of the extreme poverty in West Africa, an increase of this sort, Oxfam argues, could greatly improve the lives of West Africans.

The World Trade Organization (WTO) helps to resolve disputes among nations regarding trade issues. In 2002 Brazil, a cotton-exporting competitor of the United States, brought a case to the WTO claiming that the subsidies paid by the United States to cotton farmers (over $3 billion in 2001) violate international trade rules and distort global prices. In September 2004, the WTO sided with Brazil, finding the U.S. cotton subsidies distorting to international cotton prices. The WTO reiterated its ruling in March 2005 after the United States appealed. The United States eliminated export subsidies (financial support to increase exports) after the 2005 ruling but continued its domestic subsidies (financial support directly given to cotton farmers). In 2006, total cotton subsidies in the United States amounted to over $2.5 billion, according to the Environmental Working Group Farm Subsidy Database.

In December 2007, the WTO ruled that the United States had failed to comply with its earlier ruling that found subsidies to cotton farmers in violation of international trade rules, but the United States appealed this ruling. In June 2008, the United States lost its final appeal, with the WTO concluding that U.S. cotton subsidies breach global trade agreements. The United States continues to claim that its cotton subsidy program is not in violation of trade agreements. In August 2008, Brazil appealed for WTO sanctions of up to $4 billion against the United States.

Despite the WTO rulings, the United States continues its subsidies to cotton farmers for the time being. The Food, Conservation, and Energy Act of 2008, passed in May 2008, is largely a continuation of the 2002 Farm Bill, and continues to provide domestic subsidies to cotton farmers in the form of direct payments and other support. The Doha Development Round of WTO trade negotiations, the round of trade negotiations that began in 2001 with the purpose of lowering trade barriers, may eventually end the dispute between the United States and Brazil.

In *Opposing Viewpoints: Agricultural Subsidies*, authors explore current issues relating to agricultural subsidies in the following chapters: Why Do Agricultural Subsidies Exist? What Are Some Concerns About Agricultural Subsidies? Should Agricultural Subsidies Be Eliminated? What Are Some Alternatives to Agricultural Subsidies? The many viewpoints included in this volume demonstrate that the wide disagreement about agricultural subsidies will continue to fuel debate in the future.

OPPOSING
VIEWPOINTS®
SERIES

CHAPTER 1

Why Do Agricultural Subsidies Exist?

Chapter Preface

Agricultural subsidies are government financial supports for the agriculture industry that take a variety of forms. Agricultural subsidies can come in the form of support as varied as direct payments to farmers, disaster aid, government loans, government-supported insurance, and export advertising support. Some reasons given for various agricultural subsidies include securing the nation's food supply, helping farmers to stay in business, and ensuring high standards. In the United States, the first agricultural subsidies can be traced to legislation passed in the 1930s in response to the Great Depression.

The U.S. Department of Agriculture (USDA) is required by law to subsidize, through commodity and price supports financed by the Commodity Credit Corporation (CCC), several agricultural commodities. The permanent pieces of legislation that initially demanded these subsidies are the Agricultural Adjustment Act of 1938 and the Agricultural Act of 1949 (which together regulate supply by creating price supports and allowing the CCC to purchase surplus food), and the CCC Charter Act of 1948 (creating the CCC to act as a body responsible for stabilizing and supporting farm income and prices). Provisions of the agricultural acts are usually superseded by more current legislation, such as the current farm bill. However, whenever legislation expires and new legislation is not enacted, the law reverts back to the 1938 Act and the 1949 Act.

The Food, Conservation, and Energy Act of 2008 is the five-year farm bill passed in May 2008. Agricultural commodities protected by subsidies in the 2008 bill include wheat, corn, barley, grain sorghum, oats, upland cotton, rice, soybeans, oilseeds (sunflower seed, canola, rapeseed, safflower, flaxseed, mustard seed), and peanuts. The Congressional Budget Office (CBO) estimates the total cost of the 2008 farm bill to be $284 billion over the five-year period from 2008 to 2012. According to the Environmental Working Group's Farm Subsidy Database, USDA agricultural subsidies totaled over $177 billion in the period from 1995 to 2006. Some people worry that minor changes in the new farm bill could actually lead to an increase in subsidies, according to Dan Morgan in a May 21, 2008, *Washington Post* article.

The United States' history with agricultural subsidies is almost a century old. Whether this tradition of government support for agriculture should continue is the subject of much debate. People in favor of the subsidies claim that agricultural subsidies are necessary and that this is why they have such a long history. Those against subsidies claim either that the initial reason for agricultural subsidies has long passed or that it never applied in the first place. This chapter looks at what agricultural subsidies are and the reasons they were originally enacted.

"Domestic subsidies for agriculture are substantial and pervasive around the world, with such subsidies of all kinds totaling more than $200 billion per year."

Agricultural Subsidies Are Widespread Worldwide Governmental Supports

Congressional Budget Office (CBO)

In the following viewpoint, statistics on domestic subsidies and export subsidies are reviewed. The Congressional Budget Office (CBO) concludes that subsidies, particularly domestic subsidies, are widespread throughout the world and are substantial. The CBO argues that although the United States and the European Union provide comparable domestic subsidies based on dollar value, the domestic subsidies of the European Union are more distorting to trade. The CBO provides Congress with objective, nonpartisan, and timely analyses to aid in economic and budgetary decisions on the wide array of programs covered by the federal budget.

Congressional Budget Office (CBO), "Policies That Distort World Agricultural Trade: Prevalence and Magnitude," August 2005, p. xi, 13–37.

As you read, consider the following questions:

1. What is distinct about amber box domestic subsidies?

2. Which four countries top the list of providing domestic subsidies, in value terms?

3. Who are the top three users of export subsidies since 1998?

Subsidies by different countries can be compared in two key ways. One is to compare their absolute value when converted to some common currency; such as the dollar. That comparison is best for assessing which countries' policies most distort the total world market (although all subsidies are not equally distortionary). The other way is to calculate the subsidy rate of each country—that is, the subsidy as a percentage of the value of agricultural output—and compare such subsidy rates. That approach is better for measuring the competitive advantage a country attempts to confer on its farmers and exporters through subsidies.

Types of Support

The Uruguay Round Agreement on Agriculture [a World Trade Organization (WTO) agreement] focuses future subsidy reductions on only the most trade-distorting domestic support. It divides domestic agricultural subsidies into five categories, or "boxes": the green box, the blue box, the special and differential box, de minimis support, and the amber box. The *green box* is for measures, defined in some detail in the agreement, that were deemed by the negotiators to have little or no distorting effects on trade—that is, to have little, if any, effect on the prices and quantities of goods exported or imported (or produced, since increased production affects the prices and quantities of traded goods). The *blue box* is for certain direct payments under production-limiting programs. Such payments, while more distorting than green-box payments, are not as distorting as others and are a means some countries use to reduce the distortionary effect of their income-support programs for farmers. The *special and differential box* is for certain development subsidies granted by some developing countries. *De minimis support* consists of subsidies that are below specified percentages of the value of production that the agreement's negotiators deemed low enough so as not to be a cause for concern. The *amber box* consists of all support not falling into the other four categories. Amber-box support is generally the most distortionary of the five categories, and it is limited and reduced by the agreement. The other four categories are exempt from reduction requirements. . . .

Statistics on Domestic Subsidies

The subsidy numbers analyzed in this section are based on reports to the World Trade Organization by the various member countries as required by the Agreement on Agriculture. Both the values of the subsidies and their placement into the various boxes—green, blue, de minimis, special and differential, or amber—are (aside from conversion from foreign currency units to dollars) presented as reported by the countries, and thus their accuracy depends on the effort, judgment, and care taken by the countries in making their reports. Moreover, many countries are delinquent in their reporting, so the most recent numbers for many are several years old. Bearing those caveats in mind, one can draw a number of conclusions:

- Domestic subsidies for agriculture are substantial and pervasive around the world, with such subsidies of all kinds totaling more than $200 billion per year—roughly one-sixth of the total agricultural value added in the world—and 64 out of 76 countries reporting to the WTO that they granted subsidies of some kind in at least one of the years from 1998 through 2004.

- A few countries dominate the total dollar value of subsidies granted. The European Union and the United States each grant about one-third of the world's total—with the European Union providing a little more than the United States—and Japan provides a little less than 15 percent. Hong Kong and Singapore provide no such subsidies, and Australia grants less than one-half of 1 percent of the world's total.

- The countries with the highest rates of total subsidy—that is, total subsidies as a percentage of agricultural output—are almost entirely high-income countries. Members of the European Free Trade Association (Iceland, Norway, and Switzerland-Liechtenstein) top the list, followed by Japan, the United States, and the European Union at substantially lower but still sizable rates. Australia and New Zealand have very low rates of total subsidy.

The Distorting Subsidies

- About one-half of all domestic subsidies fall into the green box, 10 percent fall into the blue box, 5 percent are de minimis, and one-half of 1 percent fall into the special and differential box. That leaves one-third that are the distorting subsidies that fall into the amber box and are limited by the Agreement on Agriculture.

- Although the United States and the European Union provide comparable amounts of total subsidy, much more of the U.S. total falls into the green box and much less—roughly one-third as much—falls into the amber box.

- The European Union provides more than half of the world's amber-box subsidies, the United States about one-fifth, Japan about 8 percent, and all other countries substantially less.

- The countries with the highest amber-box subsidy rates are the members of the European Free Trade Association. Next is the European Union, with a substantially lower but still high rate. The United States is much farther down the list with a rate that is substantially lower than that of the European Union. Mexico and Canada have still-lower rates, and Australia's rate is very low.

- As was the case with tariffs, amber-box bounds are substantially higher than actual amber-box subsidies for most countries, so substantial reductions in those bounds will have to be negotiated in the Doha Round [WTO trade negotiation] to have much effect on actual subsidies.

- Half of all EU [European Union] amber-box subsidies in 2001 went to beef, white sugar, and butter. No product or small group of products dominated in terms of amber-box subsidy rates. Ten products had rates higher than 50 percent, and 10 additional products had rates higher than 30 percent. Among the products with such high rates were tobacco, various fruits, beef, cotton, and rice.

Countries with the Most Domestic Subsidies

Domestic subsidies for agriculture are substantial and pervasive around the world. WTO members report subsidies totaling more than $200 billion per year. Value added in the agricultural sector worldwide from 1999 through 2001 was roughly $1.2 trillion per year, so the reported subsidies were a little more than one-sixth of agricultural value added. Out of 76 countries that reported to the WTO on their domestic subsidy practices for at least one of the years from 1998 through

Total Domestic Support Reported by Countries to the World Trade Organization

(Millions of current U.S. dollars)

		Average Reported Value, 1998–2004
European Union		87,054
United States		71,337
Japan		29,053
Korea		6,120

TAKEN FROM: Congressional Budget Office, "Policies that Distort World Agricultural Trade: Prevalence and Magnitude," August 2005. www.cbo.gov.

2004, 64 reported providing subsidies of some kind—green box, blue box, special and differential box, de minimis, or amber box.

Although the practice of providing domestic subsidies is widespread, a few countries dominate in value terms. Because so many countries have not reported for a number of years, precise percentages on a current basis cannot be determined. However, the European Union and the United States each provide a little over one-third of the total provided by all countries—the EU slightly more than the United States—and Japan a little less than 15 percent. Fourth-place Korea provides only about one-quarter the amount provided by Japan—roughly 3 percent of the world's total. Hong Kong and Singapore provide no subsidies at all, and Australia provides less than half of 1 percent. . . .

Part of the reason that the European Union and the United States dominate the subsidy totals is that their economies, and in particular their agricultural sectors, are very large. When one looks at subsidy rates—that is, total subsidies as a percentage of the value of agricultural output—the picture changes. . . . Topping the list of countries for which such rates could be calculated are the members of the European Free Trade Association—Iceland, Norway, and Switzerland-Liechtenstein—with average reported rates since 1998 ranging from 140 percent down to 83 percent of their respective agricultural outputs. Japan, the United States, and the European Union each averaged 37 percent of agricultural output. U.S. neighbors Canada and Mexico were significantly lower, with averages of 12 percent and 11 percent, respectively. Australia and New Zealand averaged only 5 percent and just under 2 percent.

Breakdown of Subsidies by WTO Category

As noted above in the discussion of the Uruguay Round Agreement on Agriculture, not all subsidies are created equal when it comes to their distortion of output and trade, and the agreement makes allowance for that with its green box, blue box, amber box, and other support measures. Roughly half of all reported domestic subsidies around the world fall into the green box, which is reserved for subsidies deemed to have little, if any, distortionary effect on output or trade. Another 10 percent fall into the blue-box category, which is reserved for certain support payments linked to production-limiting programs. Only the European Union, Japan, Norway, the Czech Republic, the Slovak Republic, Slovenia, and Estonia have made use of the blue box.

About 5 percent of all subsidies fall into the de minimis category. Those subsidies can, in principle, be distortionary, but their distortionary effect is limited by the fact that they are less than 5 percent of the value of the product being subsidized. Subsidies in the special and differential box also can be distortionary, but they constitute only about one-half of 1 percent of all subsidies. Hence, for the world market as a whole, they are not very significant in comparison with the other categories (although they may indeed be significant to some of the countries that make use of them). Excluding all of the preceding categories leaves roughly one-third of all subsidies worldwide falling into the amber box, ranging from $78 billion to $80 billion in 1998 and 1999 down to a little less than $65 billion in 2001 when rough corrections are made for significant nonreporting countries. Those are the subsidies that most distort trade and that therefore were limited and reduced by the Agreement on Agriculture.

Individual countries vary substantially from the proportions for the world as a whole, with significant implications for the relative distortion caused by the countries' policies and for the treatment of their policies by the Agreement on Agriculture. Of particular note are the different proportions of the European Union and the United States. As noted above, the European Union and the United States provide comparable amounts of domestic subsidies (summing over all categories) in dollar-value terms—the European Union granting a slightly larger amount of subsidies but also having a slightly larger agricultural output, with the result that the EU subsidy rate is very close to that of the United States. However, roughly 70 percent of U.S. subsidies fall into the green box and a little under 10 percent fall into the de minimis category, leaving only slightly more than 20 percent that are the amber-box subsidies that distort trade and are limited by the Agreement on Agriculture. At the same time, only about one-quarter of EU subsidies fall into the green box, and only a little more than one-half of 1 percent fall into the de minimis category. Consequently, even with roughly one-quarter of its subsidies falling into the blue box, one-half of EU subsidies still fall into the amber box. As a result, the European Union has three times the dollar value of amber-box subsidies that the United States has. . . .

Statistics on Export Subsidies

Export subsidies are more distorting to international trade than any other kind of subsidy, a fact that is reflected in the way they are treated by the Agreement on Agriculture. The agreement placed little or no restriction on several categories of domestic subsidies—the green box, the blue box, and the other support measures. However, it required reduction commitments for all export subsidies covered by the agreement.

Although the agreement made a temporary exception for developing countries without export-subsidy-reduction commitments to provide certain kinds of export subsidies during the agreement's initial nine-year implementation period, that period is now over [in 2005].The only export subsidies now allowed and subject to negotiation in the Doha Round are those subject to reduction commitments made under the Uruguay Round Agreement on Agriculture. Therefore, the discussion in this section is restricted to those subsidies, and the temporary subsidies reported under the exception for developing countries are ignored. The major conclusions are:

- Export subsidies are much less widespread than are domestic subsidies, with only 25 countries having subsidy-reduction commitments and two of those commitments having a final bound value of zero.

- The European Union dominates the use of export subsidies even more than it does the use of domestic subsidies, providing 85 percent to 90 percent of all the export subsidies reported to the World Trade Organization by countries with reduction commitments. Ranking next is Switzerland-Liechtenstein, with 4.5 percent to 6.5 percent of the world's total, followed by Norway and the United States with 1 percent to 2 percent.

- The highest export subsidy rates are those by Switzerland-Liechtenstein and the European Union—no other country even comes close. The United States has a very low subsidy rate that places it well down in the rankings.

- As was the case with tariffs and amber-box subsidies, export subsidy bindings are substantially higher than actual export subsidies for many countries. However, that fact has less significance for the Doha Round than does the corresponding fact for tariffs and amber-box subsidies because the framework agreement calls for export subsidies to be eliminated.

- The EU products receiving the greatest dollar value of export subsidies are dairy products, sugar, and beef.

Countries with the Most Export Subsidies

Export subsidies are used disproportionately by European countries, especially the high-income European countries.... The top three users of such subsidies since 1998 measured by dollar value have been the European Union, Switzerland-Liechtenstein, and Norway. The United States took fourth place.

The European Union granted between 85 percent and 90 percent of the total export subsidies reported to the WTO in each of the years from 1998 through 2002 (the most recent year for which it has reported). Adding in the rest of Europe brings the total up to well over 95 percent, even with Turkey, Cyprus, and Iceland excluded. The United States ranged between 0.5 percent and 2.25 percent.

Although the total value of U.S. export subsidies is much smaller than that of the European Union, they nevertheless cause distortions in certain product markets. Those distortions have raised concerns among foreign competitors and have led to challenges to some U.S. export subsidies in the WTO....

When export subsidies are expressed as a percentage of the value of exports, Switzerland-Liechtenstein jumps above the European Union, with subsidies equal to 9.3 percent of total export value compared with the EU's 6.6 percent.... The latter takes a strong second place, however. The Czech Republic and Norway are a distant third and fourth place at 1.6 percent. U.S. subsidies are only 0.1 percent of total export value, and Australia's are only 0.004 percent. (A lack of data on the value of exports prevented the computation of subsidy rates for Cyprus, Mexico, the Slovak Republic, Panama, and Venezuela, so it is unclear where they would fall in the ranking.)

It should be noted that most countries do not subsidize all exports—only certain products. The subsidy rates for those products might be significantly higher than the average rate for all agricultural exports of the country.

> "The Farm Bill emerged as one of the most ambitious social, cultural, and economic programs ever attempted by the U.S. government."

U.S. Agricultural Subsidies Are the Result of the Great Depression

Daniel Imhoff

In the following viewpoint, Daniel Imhoff traces the history of the origin of federal farm support programs, which include agricultural subsidies. Imhoff claims that the farm crisis of the 1930s, brought on by the Great Depression, led to the emergence of a federal farm bill that sought to create a centralized food policy. The author argues that this federal food policy has been a source of controversy ever since. Daniel Imhoff is a researcher, author, and independent publisher, and is the author of Food Fight: The Citizen's Guide to a Food and Farm Bill.

As you read, consider the following questions:

1. During the Great Depression, what percentage of Americans lived on farms?

2. The first farm bill emerged as a cornerstone of which American president's agenda?

3. According to Imhoff, in the early years of the Farm Bill, were programs designed to relieve hunger successful?

The ideal of a nation built on the sweat and sacrifice of hard-working, God-fearing farmers taps a deep nerve in the American psyche. In 1801, when Thomas Jefferson became the United States' third president, 95 percent of the population made their full-time living from agriculture. Jefferson envisioned the United States as a democracy orbiting around a citizenry of yeomen farmers. He wrote:

> Cultivators of the earth are the most valuable citizens. They are the most vigorous, the most independent, the most virtuous and they are tied to the country and wedded to its liberty and interests by the most lasting bonds. I think our governments will remain virtuous for many centuries so long as they are chiefly agricultural.

Half a century later, Abraham Lincoln planted the seeds of this vision with the establishment of the railroad land grants, the Land Grant College system, and the Homestead Act, all intended to spread independence, settlement, and stability. As the decades wore on, wave upon wave of immigrants determined to strike it rich exploited the continent's resources and natural heritage, bringing with them crops, domesticated livestock, and farming methods often not well suited to the land. By the early decades of the twentieth century, just 45 percent of the population lived on farms, and it was becoming clear that pioneering an agrarian democracy was problematic. But it took the Dust Bowl and the Great Depression to bring on total collapse.

The Farm Crisis

America during the Great Depression was a hungry nation, whose most valuable natural resource—the soil—was literally blowing away in catastrophic fashion. On a single Sunday afternoon in 1935, for example, a storm barreling through the Texas Panhandle swept 300,000 tons of topsoil into the air, choking people and animals, blanketing houses and cars, and ravaging the countryside. This one event carried twice the volume of soil excavated during the entire construction of the Panama Canal.

During this time, more than a third of the U.S. population was eking out a subsistence of grinding poverty. One in four Americans still lived on farms. Increasing numbers of tenant farmers and sharecroppers were forced from their land or pushed into desperate poverty. Farm foreclosures had become commonplace. In the cities, a domino effect of bank closures and bank holidays threatened financial meltdown, while soup and bread lines grew ever longer.

By most accounts, the United States was becoming a cauldron of civil unrest. Drought, searing heat, dust storms, floods, inadequate minimum wages, maximum hours, child labor abuse and working conditions in industry, monopolistic and unfair business practices had taken a punishing toll. In *The Grapes of Wrath*, John Steinbeck described the situation this way:

> And the dispossessed, the migrants, flowed into California, two hundred and fifty thousand, and three hundred thousand. Behind them new tractors were going on the land and the tenants were being forced off. And new waves were on the way, new waves of the dispossessed and homeless, hard, intent, and dangerous . . .

Ironically, the farm crisis of the 1930s was triggered not by too little food, but by too much. A decade of overzealous and speculative planting, combined with technological advances such as tractors and nitrogen fertilizers synthesized from natural gas, had yielded chronic overproduction in most crops. The "parity"—or disparity, as it were—between low farm prices and the higher costs of manufactured goods reached an

A Temporary Solution

Franklin Roosevelt's Administration started farm aid in response to the Dust Bowl and the Depression, calling it "a temporary solution to deal with an emergency." But in Washington, the emergency has never ended. The government still gives farmers your money—more than ever over the past decade—along with research projects to expand their yields, restoration projects to clean up their messes, flood-control and irrigation projects to protect and enhance their land, visa programs to supply them with cheap labor, ethanol mandates and tariffs to boost their prices, and tax breaks by the bushel.

Michael Grunwald, "Why Our Farm Policy Is Failing,"
Time, *November 12, 2007.*

ever-widening gap. While low crop prices directly benefited distributors, processors, and monopolists who were increasingly dominating the food system, the U.S. agrarian culture and economy was unraveling. In order to stay afloat in a global economy, farmers planted more and more acreage. But this resulted in glutted markets, further land abuse, and prices far below the costs of production. Total farm income fell by two-thirds between 1929 and 1932. Six of every ten farms had been mortgaged to survive, and many did not. In the single year of 1932, five of every one hundred farms in Iowa were foreclosed and sold at auction. Then in 1933, the price of corn actually plummeted to zero—as grain elevators simply stopped buying surplus corn altogether.

The Farm Bill

In the face of such extraordinary circumstances, the Farm Bill emerged as one of the most ambitious social, cultural, and economic programs ever attempted by the U.S. government. One of the cornerstones of Franklin Roosevelt's New Deal agenda, and administered by Secretary of Agriculture Henry A. Wallace, the early Farm Bill responded directly to a number of crises:

- Rock bottom crop prices due to overproduction;

- Widespread hunger and social inequalities;

- Catastrophic erosion and soil loss due to prolonged drought and poor land stewardship practices;

- Lack of credit and insurance available to subsistence farmers;

- Need for electricity, water, and basic infrastructure in rural communities;

- Unfair export policies prohibiting free and fair trade;

- Increasing civil unrest.

Centralized food policy was not a novel concept. The Romans created a welfare system that included the distribution of free bread and grains. Their bread allotment program, which continued for centuries, was a calculated measure to stave off mob revolts. It was also only made possible by out sourcing. Rome depended almost entirely on Egyptian farmers for its wheat.

Federal Support Programs

Henry Wallace was a gifted, lifelong farmer, a vegetarian, and spiritual seeker, whose father had also been a Secretary of Agriculture. Under Wallace's direction, the USDA [U.S. Department of Agriculture] blossomed into one of the largest arms of the government, with more than 146,000 employees and a budget of more than $1 billion. (USDA Farm Bill budgets now average nearly $90 billion.) One of the driving principles of Wallace's administration was the creation of a farm support program based on a concept known as the "Ever-Normal Granary." This initiative took its historical precedent from ancient times, traceable to both Confucian China and the biblical story of Joseph. The idea was straightforward though politically challenging. The government would purchase and stockpile surplus crops and livestock during good years as a protection against dwindling supply in lean times. This helped to accomplish two important goals: (1) raising market prices for farmers by contracting supply; and (2) distributing meat and grain products in times of need.

In addition, farmers participating in federally supported programs were required to idle a certain percentage of their historical base acreage, in an attempt to prevent overproduction. Author Michael Pollan describes how these price support programs worked to regulate markets:

> For storable commodities such as corn, the government established a target price based on the cost of production, and whenever the market price dropped below the target, the farmer was given a choice. Instead of dumping the corn into a weak market (thereby weakening it further), the farmer could take out a loan from the government—using his crop as collateral—that allowed him to store his grain until prices recovered. At that point he sold the corn and paid back the loan; if corn prices stayed low, he could elect to keep the money he'd borrowed and, in repayment, give the government his corn, which would then go into something that came to be called, rather quaintly, the "Ever-Normal Granary."

Government involvement in the food system did not begin and end with price supports and grain warehousing. Wallace's vision for farm policy included a range of departments and programs that, taken together, combined to make up an integrated food, farming, and stewardship platform. The Soil Conservation Service (originally the Soil Erosion Service and today the Natural Resources Conservation Service) addressed erosion control with alternative methods of tillage, cover cropping, crop rotation, and fertilization. Land use planning incentives were enacted to regulate crop acreage and maximize the fallowing and recovery of fields. Programs were specifically tailored to assist sharecroppers and the rural poor. Credit and crop insurance programs provided financial mechanisms in response to the early and late season needs of farmers. Research into plant and animal diseases and new varieties and uses of crops pressed for critical innovations. Food relief and school lunch programs were part of an overall policy to provide a baseline of hunger and nutritional assistance.

Ongoing Controversy

Despite a demonstrated seven-times "multiplier effect" that every government dollar spent generated in the overall economy, New Deal agriculture reforms were controversial from the outset. Many farmers considered hunger relief both a shameful charity and a threat to free markets. As a consequence, in the early years of the Farm Bill, millions of young hogs purchased by the government to restrict supply (bump up prices) and feed the hungry never reached their intended beneficiaries. Instead they were slaughtered and dumped in the Missouri River. Likewise, millions of gallons of milk were poured into the streets rather than nourishing famished and distended bellies. Not until the term *relief* was stricken from the titles of food distribution programs and replaced with the Federal Surplus Commodities Corporation were they ultimately accepted by powerful farmer coalitions. In 1936, the Supreme Court declared that initial programs to limit acreage and set target prices for upland cotton were unconstitutional, though marketing loans and deficiency payments were later upheld.

Farmers themselves seem to have been conflicted about this emerging agricultural order and over the years have been co-opted and manipulated by more powerful interests. Historian Bernard DeVito wrote that "farmers throughout the West were always demanding further government help and then furiously denouncing the government for paternalism, and trying to avoid regulation." A decade prior to the 1930s Farm Bill programs, H.L. Mencken said of American farmers, "When the going is good for him he robs the rest of us up to the extreme limit of our endurance; when the going is bad, he comes up bawling for help out of the public till. . . . There has never been a time, in good season or bad, when his hands were not itching for more."

Henry Wallace, meanwhile, moved on to become vice president during the second term of Franklin Roosevelt, and his vision for farm and food policy was never integrated as he had envisioned. A genuine attempt had been made to enact policies that brought balanced abundance to the people, protected against shortages (a significant foresight considering what transpired during World War II), and buffered farmers against losses with loan and insurance programs. Ultimately, however, these programs could not solve one of agriculture's biggest challenges of the twentieth century: overproduction in a rapidly globalizing and industrializing food system.

> "In addition to routine cash subsidies, the USDA provides subsidized crop insurance, marketing support, and other services for farm businesses."

U.S. Agricultural Subsidies Are the Result of a Wide Variety of Governmental Programs

Chris Edwards

In the following viewpoint, Chris Edwards claims that agricultural subsidies have only grown since their advent over a century ago, despite a lack of obvious benefits. Edwards delineates eight types of farm subsidies, which include direct payments as well as indirect support. Types of indirect government subsidies for farm ers include loans, insurance, export subsidies, and agricultural research. Chris Edwards is director of tax policy studies at the Cato Institute and author of Downsizing the Federal Government.

As you read, consider the following questions:

1. According to the author, in 2002 did Congress increase or decrease the amount of future agricultural subsidies?

2. In what two ways do marketing loans encourage over-production, according to Edwards?

3. How does the federal government subsidize farmers' yield and revenue insurance, according to the author?

The USDA [U.S. Department of Agriculture] distributes between $10 billion and $30 billion in cash subsidies to farmers and owners or farmland each year. The particular amount depends on market prices for crops, the level of disaster payments, and other factors. More than 90 percent of agriculture subsidies go to farmers of five crops—wheat, corn, soybeans, rice, and cotton. Roughly a million farmers and landowners receive subsidies, but the payments are heavily tilted toward the largest producers.

In addition to routine cash subsidies, the USDA provides subsidized crop insurance, marketing support, and other services for farm businesses. The USDA also performs extensive agricultural research and generates statistical data for the industry. These indirect subsidies and services cost taxpayers about $5 billion each year, putting total farm support at between $15 billion and $35 billion annually.

The History of Subsidies

Agriculture has long attracted federal government support. The first subsidy program for agriculture was the Morrill Act of 1862, which established the land-grant colleges. That was followed by the Hatch Act of 1887, which funded agricultural research, and by the Smith-Lever Act of 1914, which funded agriculture education. Still, the subsidies remained small, and until the 1930s the USDA's agriculture efforts were mainly focused on producing statistics, funding research, and responding to problems such as pest infestations.

A large array of farm subsidy programs was enacted during the 1930s, beginning with the Agriculture Adjustment Act of 1933. New Deal programs included commodity price supports and production controls, marketing orders to limit competition, import barriers, and crop insurance. The particular structures of farm programs have changed over time, but the central planning philosophies behind them have changed little in seven decades. Dozens of other industries have been deregulated and opened to domestic and global competition in recent decades. But agricultural policies remain stuck in the 1930s, despite the failures of those policies.

Between the 1940s and the 1980s, Congress occasionally considered farm reforms, usually when commodity prices were high, but then it reverted to subsidy increases when market conditions were less favorable. The Reagan administration proposed serious cuts to farm subsidies, but farm finances were in bad shape in the 1980s, which prompted Congress to increase farm support. Sometimes Congress has changed course when its policies have created obvious disasters, such as the massive crop stockpiles built up in 1960 as a result of overproduction in the 1950s.

Against Current Subsidies

Agriculture subsidies have never made economic sense, but since the 1930s, farmers have resisted changes to subsidy programs, and they have generally held sway in Congress. While farmers are a smaller share of the population today than in the 1930s, the farm lobby is perhaps as strong as ever. One reason is that farm-state legislators have co-opted the support of urban legislators, who seek increased subsidies in agriculture bills for programs such as food stamps. Legislators interested in rural environmental subsidies have also been co-opted as supporters of farm bills. Thus many legislators have an interest in increasing the USDA's budget, but there are few opposing them on behalf of the taxpayer.

In 1996 Congress did enact some pro-market agriculture reforms under the "Freedom to Farm" law. The law allowed farmers greater flexibility in their planting decisions and moved toward greater reliance on market supply and demand. But the law did not cut farm subsidies, and Congress expanded subsidies in a series of large supplemental farm bills in the late 1990s. When the 1996 law was passed, subsidies were expected to cost $47 billion in total from 1996 to 2002, but subsidies ended up costing $121 billion. Republican farm policies have been a disaster from the taxpayers' point of view.

That was reaffirmed in 2002 when Congress, with the support of the [George W.] Bush administration, passed farm legislation that partly reversed the few reforms of 1996. The 2002 law increased projected subsidy payments by 74 percent over 10 years. It added new crops to the subsidy rolls and created a new price guarantee scheme called the "countercyclical" program. Congress is scheduled to reauthorize farm subsidy programs in 2007 [the farm subsidy programs were continued by the passage of the Food, Conservation, and Energy Act of 2008].

The extensive federal welfare system for farm businesses is costly to taxpayers and creates distortions in markets. Subsidies induce farmers to overproduce, which pushes down prices and creates demands for further subsidies. Subsidies inflate land prices in rural America. And the flow of subsidies and regulations from Washington hinders farmers from innovating, cutting costs, diversifying their land use, and taking the actions needed to prosper in a competitive global economy.

The distortions caused by federal farm policies have long been recognized. In 1932 a member of Congress noted that the Agriculture Department spent "hundreds of millions a year to stimulate the production of farm products by every method, from irrigating waste lands to loaning and even giving money to the farmers, and simultaneously advising them that there is no adequate market for their crops, and that they should restrict production." the folly is the same seven decades later, except that the subsidies have increased from "hundreds of millions" to tens of billions of dollars.

Complex Policy

Farm policy is extraordinarily complex. This complexity conveniently insulates the farm policymaking process within a small group of lawmakers and interest groups who specialize in the details.

Subsidy eligibility is based on the crop. More than 90 percent of all subsidies go to just five crops—wheat, cotton, corn, soybeans, and rice—while the vast majority of crops are ineligible for subsidies. Once eligibility is established, subsidies are paid per amount of the crop produced, so the largest farms automatically receive the largest checks.

Subsidies are also quite duplicative. The names of the three different commodity subsidies do not adequately describe their purposes:

- *Marketing loan program.* Despite being called a "loan," this program has the net effect of reimbursing farmers for the difference between a crop's market price and the minimum level that Congress sets every five to six years.

- *Fixed payments.* Fixed payments are given to farmers based on their farms' historical production and are unrelated to actual production.

- *Countercyclical payments.* This program functions somewhat similarly to the marketing loan program by subsidizing farmers up to a government-set target price. This rate is higher than the marketing loan rate and therefore represents an additional subsidy.

Brian M. Riedl, "How Farm Subsidies Harm Taxpayers, Consumers, and Farmers, Too," Backgrounder, June 19, 2007.

Eight Types of Farm Subsidy

1. Direct Payments. "Direct" payments are federal cash subsidies for producers of 10 crops: wheat, corn, sorghum, barley, oats, cotton, rice, soybeans, minor oilseeds, and peanuts. The last three were added in the 2002 farm law. Direct payments are based on a historical measure of a farm's acres used for production and are not related to current production or prices.

Established in 1996, direct payments were intended to be transitional, a way to wean farmers from old-fashioned price guarantee programs. Unfortunately, direct payments have not been phased down over time as planned. In most years, direct payments are the largest source of subsidies to farmers at more than $5 billion annually.

The fact that direct payments are decoupled from current production reduces economic distortions. However, it is creating a growing scandal because large subsidies are being paid to owners of land that is no longer used for farming. The *Washington Post* estimated that between 2000 and 2006 the USDA handed out $1.3 billion in direct payments to people who don't farm. The newspaper points to thousands of acres of land formerly used for growing rice in Texas. The land is now used for nonfarming purposes, such as suburban housing, but the landowners continue to receive federal farm subsidies.

2. Marketing Loans. The marketing loan program is a price support program that has been a key part of the farm subsidy system since the New Deal. Originally just a short-term loan program, today it provides large subsidies by paying guaranteed minimum prices for crops. The marketing loan program encourages overproduction both by setting a price floor for crops and by reducing the price variability that would otherwise face producers in normal open markets.

The marketing loan program covers the same crops as the direct subsidy program—wheat, corn, sorghum, barley, oats, cotton, rice, soybeans, minor oilseeds, and peanuts. But, in addition, the 2002 farm law expanded eligibility for marketing loans to producers of wool, mohair, honey, dry peas, lentils, and chickpeas. In recent years, payments under this program ranged from about $1 billion to $7 billion annually.

Under the program, farmers take "nonrecourse" loans from the USDA using their crops as collateral, which allows farmers to default on the loans without penalty. In the past, if market prices fell below target levels, farmers kept their loans and forfeited their low-value crop to the government. Taxpayers were stuck paying the loan costs and the costs of storing government crop stockpiles. But today, most marketing loan subsidies are in the form of "loan deficiency payments," which allow farmers to bypass the loan process and simply receive a subsidy payment. Alternatively, farmers can receive "marketing loan gains," under which farmers can repay their USDA loans at preferential rates.

Farmers don't receive subsidies from the marketing loan program just when crop prices are low. They have become expert at gaming the system to maximize their subsidies every year. Farmers can lock in high government benefits when seasonal prices are low and wait until market prices are higher to sell their crops. The *Washington Post* reports that "growers reap benefits even in the good years," noting that the program "has become so ingrained in farmland finances that farmers sometimes wish for market prices to drop so they can capture a larger subsidy."

3. Countercyclical Payments. While the 1996 farm law moved away from traditional price guarantee subsidies, the 2002 farm bill embraced them with the addition of the countercyclical program. This program covers the same commodities as the direct payments program—wheat, corn, sorghum, barley, oats, cotton, rice, soybeans, minor oilseeds, and peanuts. In recent years, countercyclical payments have ranged from about $1 billion to $4 billion annually.

The countercyclical program provides larger subsidies when market prices are lower. It also stimulates excess farm production, as does the marketing loan program. However, countercyclical payments are tied to a measure of historical production, whereas marketing loan subsidies are tied to current production. For that reason, countercyclical payments are thought to be less distortionary than marketing loan payments.

4. Conservation Subsidies. USDA conservation programs dispense about $3 billion annually to the nation's farmers. The largest conservation subsidy program is the Conservation Reserve Program [CRP], which was created in 1985 to idle millions of acres of farmland. Under CRP, farmers are paid on a per acre basis, not to grow crops, but to cultivate ground cover, such as grass or trees, on retired acres. About one-third of land idled under the CRP is owned by retired farmers, thus one does not even have to be a working farmer to get these subsidies.

The USDA provides a range of other conservation subsidy programs, including the Conservation Security Program, which was added in 2002. These programs respond to the problem that farm subsidies cause overproduction on marginal farmland. But an easier and cheaper way to reduce overproduction would be to simply eliminate all farm subsidies.

5. Insurance. The Risk Management Agency [RMA] runs the USDA's farm insurance programs. Both "yield" and "revenue" insurance are available to farmers to protect against adverse weather, pests, and low market prices. The RMA describes its mission as helping farmers "manage their business risks through effective, market-based risk management solutions." The RMA has annual outlays of about $3.4 billion and employs about 550 people, and its activities are far from "market-based."

Federal crop insurance policies are sold and serviced by 16 private insurance companies, which receive federal subsidies for their administrative costs and insurance risks. The firms operate like a cartel, earning excess profits from the high premiums they charge. They get away with that because the government provides large subsidies for insurance premiums, such that farmers pay only about one-third the full cost of their policies. The cartel-like structure of the current system was made clear in 2005, when, under lobbying pressure from insurance companies, Congress derailed an attempt by a company to offer discount insurance policies to farmers.

In 2007, USDA crop insurance programs were heavily criticized at a rare oversight hearing on an agriculture program by a non-agriculture committee of Congress. The chairman of the House Oversight and Government Reform Committee, Henry Waxman (D-CA), called USDA insurance "a textbook example of waste, fraud, and abuse in federal spending . . . over $8 billion in taxpayer funds have been squandered in excess payments to insurers and other middlemen." Time will tell whether the agriculture committees in Congress will heed Waxman's calls for reform.

6. Disaster Aid. Federal crop insurance is not available for all commodities. For products that are not covered by federal insurance, such as aquaculture, mushrooms, Christmas trees, ginseng, and turf grasses, the government pays for losses through the Noninsured Crop Disaster Assistance Program. This program was enacted in 1984 and expanded in 2000.

Whether or not farmers are covered by insurance, they can be sure that Congress will rush to pass an "emergency" relief bill after even the slightest adverse event. Congress frequently passes farm disaster bills, and these are substantial sources of subsidies for farmers. A *Washington Post* analysis found that "farmers often get paid twice by the government, once in subsidized insurance and then again in disaster assistance."

Over the decades, Congress has repeatedly expanded crop insurance programs to supposedly reduce farmers' dependence on emergency bailouts. But both insurance subsidies and disaster aid keep growing. After just about any damage to any crop, Congress jumps in to declare a "disaster" and distribute millions of dollars to farmers, regardless of whether farmers are insured, and often regardless of whether farmers sustained substantial damage.

7. *Export Subsidies.* The USDA operates a range of programs to aid farmers and food companies in their foreign sales. The Market Access Program hands out about $140 million annually to producers in support of activities such as advertising campaigns. Recipients include the Distilled Spirits Council, the Pet Food Institute, the Association of Brewers, the Popcorn Board, the Wine Institute, and Welch's Food. Another program, the Foreign Market Development program, hands out $35 million annually to groups such as the American Peanut Council, the Cotton Council International, and the Mohair Council of America. The 2002 farm law substantially increased funding for export subsidy programs.

8. *Agricultural Research and Statistics.* Most American industries fund their own research and development programs. The agriculture industry is a notable exception. The USDA spends about $3 billion annually on agricultural research, statistical information services, and economic studies. The USDA carries out research in 108 different locations and provides subsidies to the 50 states for research and education.

| "Low prices triggered high subsidies in the US, not the reverse, as many believe."

Agricultural Subsidies Are a Response to Low Prices

Daryll E. Ray, Daniel G. De La Torre Ugarte, and Kelly J. Tiller

In the following viewpoint, Daryll E. Ray, Daniel G. De La Torre Ugarte, and Kelly J. Tiller argue that agricultural subsidies are the result of low prices. The authors contend that the continued lowering of prices for crops is due to the policy shift toward freer markets that has reduced price supports and supply control programs. Daryll E. Ray, Daniel G. De La Torre Ugarte, and Kelly J. Tiller are professors and members of the Agricultural Policy Analysis Center at the University of Tennessee.

As you read, consider the following questions:

1. According to the authors, the traditional role of the federal government is to do what for agriculture?

Daryll E. Ray, Daniel G. De La Torre Ugarte, and Kelly J. Tiller, From *Rethinking US Agricultural Policy: Changing Course to Secure Farmer Livelihoods Worldwide.* Agricultural Policy Analysis Center (APAC), 2003. Copyright © 2003 University of Tennessee, Institute of Agriculture—Agricultural Policy Analysis Center. Reproduced by permission.

2. Since the mid-1980s, according to the authors, the United States has attempted to do what to increase U.S. competitiveness in export markets?

3. Beginning in 1998, subsidies to farmers increased by what percent over subsidies from 1990 to 1997, according to the authors?

The primary lesson to be gathered from the history of US farm policy is that agricultural markets do not tend to self-correct. Rather, when prices are low, production does not decline enough on its own. Nor does domestic demand or even export demand increase enough to rebalance markets and allow farmers to earn a living—that is, a profit—from selling their products.

Agricultural Policy History

US agricultural policy has heavily influenced two important aspects of US crop agriculture: growth in its capacity to produce and the proportion of productive capacity used.

From its birth as a nation, the US pursued policies that promoted phenomenal growth in productive capacity, supported by the taxpaying public. In the 19th century, government chose to expand the frontier by distributing land to would-be farmers virtually free of charge.

Once most of the land was put into production, US taxpayers bankrolled a system of research stations and extension services to generate and disseminate new technologies. The system has been a tremendous success. It continues to ensure that each new generation of Americans will have access to ample quantities of safe food at reasonable prices.

The other side of the coin is that publicly sponsored research and extension services contribute to price and income problems. Clearly, neither the US nor the rest of the world would be facing today's low prices and failing small farms if the cumulative growth in agricultural productivity had not taken place.

From the 1930s through most of the 20th century, US policies included a variety of programs that address the price and income problems arising out of our immense and fully utilized productive capacity. Most programs involved some combination of income support, price support and stabilization, production management, demand enhancement, import restriction, or conservation. . . .

The capacity to produce is not a mandate to use it fully. For example, in the manufacturing sector, between 15 and 25 percent of productive capacity is intentionally idled at any given time by reason of market supply and demand conditions. But unlike firms in other industries, individual crop farmers do not have the ability to influence the total supply of output. Nor have farmers been successful in organizing self-help supply management schemes to adjust output to the needs of the market.

Thus, the traditional role of the federal government was to do for agriculture what it could not do for itself: manage productive capacity to provide sustainable and stable prices and incomes. Until the mid-1980s (and beyond, in some cases), the primary focus of US agricultural policy was on production management programs and price support and stabilization programs.

Production Management Programs

In effect, the Secretary of Agriculture decided how much productive capacity should be left unused each year. The government employed several devices to manage supply, but usually farmers were asked to idle various amounts of acreage. Such an approach is far from exact. For one thing, in contrast to manufacturing tractors, where the number to be built can change daily or weekly, the Secretary of Agriculture has only one opportunity per year to influence how productive capacity is to be used for next year's crop. Factors such as weather and slippage resulting from the idling of the least productive land make estimating annual production a very difficult process.

But even if mistakes occurred, adjustments could be made the following year, and the market was aware of this option. So if, in a given year, yields were high, inventories increased, and prices declined, the market responded to the high probability that a set-aside would be imposed the next crop year. Without a set-aside or similar mechanism, crop demanders will delay purchases in a high-yield year because they believe that crop prices will be as low or lower again next year.

Despite their built-in complications, supply management policies have historically prevented the chronic overproduction and depressed prices that would have occurred from a full use of agriculture's productive capacity all the time.

Price Support Programs

Price support programs put a floor under major-crop prices. So if the Secretary erred in setting aside too little acreage because of above-average yields or unusually low demand, prices were prevented from plummeting uncontrollably. The price floor was equal to the loan rate for a crop, that is, the per unit value of the crop used as collateral under a government loan. For example, if the government values a crop of 1,000 bushels of corn at a loan rate of $2 per bushel, the price floor for the crop would be $2. When the loan comes due, the farmer could "give" the grain to the government in full payment of the principal and interest on his loan, thereby receiving the $2 loan rate as the "price" for his crop. If the market price were above the loan rate plus interest, the farmer had the option of paying off the loan, plus interest, and selling his crop at the higher market price. The use of a high loan rate, especially if there are no means to manage supply, can lead to an excessive accumulation of government stocks, along with expensive storage costs.

Policy Shift Toward Freer Markets

Over the last two decades, the goal to ensure growth in productive capacity has remained, but the protection of prices and farmer incomes through managing the capacity has not. Rather, the government has placed its reliance on the free market to determine prices and to make direct payments to support farmer incomes during times of low prices. To absorb excess inventory, US policy shifted away from production management and price support and toward demand expansion—especially export demand. Advocates of freer markets and trade liberalization were successful in persuading policy makers to encourage lower prices by reducing crop price supports, expecting that a barrage of exports would follow. It was expected that by modifying the "government intervention" of price supports, the US agricultural sector would quickly adjust to the greater export volume and farmers would reap the benefits of the export boom.

Since the mid-1980s, the United States has deliberately attempted to reduce market prices for commodities in pursuit of increasing US competitiveness in export markets. Emphasis on trade liberalization and the need to comply with international trade agreements further contributed to full-scale endorsement of this objective.

Despite the popular misconception among economic experts that these policies have been the source of great export growth, exports have not generally increased at all. The export boom did not materialize. . . .

When the export boom did not occur, proponents of freer markets argued that the remaining government price support and supply control programs were putting a crimp on exports. In fact, a growing number of economists held the belief that commodity programs were relics of the past. It was assumed that because agriculture is less of a force in the economy today (only 2 percent of the population lives on farms, as compared with 25 percent in the 1930s), farmers are more likely to respond to low prices because they purchase more of their fertilizer and fuel rather than produce it on the farm. This thinking led gradually to the conclusion that government intervention in the agriculture sector was no longer needed. It was thought that intervention was a hindrance to realizing the full income potential of the agriculture sector. At the same time that conventional wisdom about the price responsiveness of the agricultural sector was shifting, the agribusiness lobby was gaining power and influence. The growing influence of the agribusiness lobby has outpaced that of grassroots farm organizations.

The result of this thinking was the 1996 Farm Bill, which removed all vestiges of government price supports and annual supply controls. The 1996 Farm Bill was debated and passed during a period of very high prices and high optimism for growth in the US agricultural sector. In 1995, prices of most major crops—corn, wheat, cotton, grain sorghum, oats, and barley prices—were at their all-time record highs. The high prices were primarily a result of tight world markets, compounded by weather conditions in the US that resulted in 1995 yields that were well below trend levels. At the time, USDA forecasters were projecting tremendous growth in US crop exports for the foreseeable future.

Exports of soybeans, and especially cotton, did increase and actually exceeded projections during recent years. But that was not the case for most other crops.... [T]he trend of US exports for the eight major crops taken together continued to be flat after 1996. The skyward export trend in the 1970s, while perhaps burned into minds, does not reflect recent reality. Domestic demand, which has grown faster than US popu-

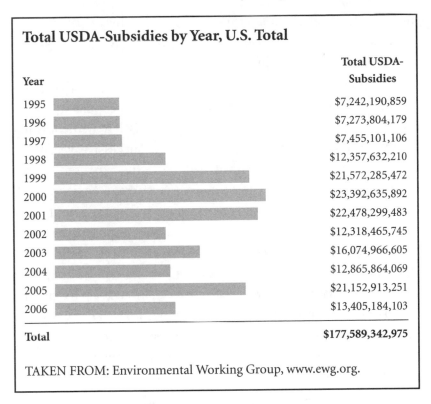

Total USDA-Subsidies by Year, U.S. Total

Year		Total USDA-Subsidies
1995		$7,242,190,859
1996		$7,273,804,179
1997		$7,455,101,106
1998		$12,357,632,210
1999		$21,572,285,472
2000		$23,392,635,892
2001		$22,478,299,483
2002		$12,318,465,745
2003		$16,074,966,605
2004		$12,865,864,069
2005		$21,152,913,251
2006		$13,405,184,103
Total		**$177,589,342,975**

TAKEN FROM: Environmental Working Group, www.ewg.org.

lation because of non-food demand, has been the driving force for major-crop demand for the last quarter century.

Low Prices and Subsidies

With the removal of the set-aside program, acreage previously withheld from production was freed up. With no mechanisms for acreage reduction to manage supply, the immediate response was an increase in crop acreage. It was no surprise that acreage planted to the eight major crops increased over six percent (over 15 million acres) the year the set-aside policy was removed. Inventory adjustments and world conditions staved off massive price declines, but only until 1998. Thereafter prices plummeted, and government subsidies ballooned to compensate for lost market income. Even as prices declined, the previously idled acreage that came into production in 1996 remained in cultivation. Since 1996, the indexed market price for the eight major crops has declined by nearly 40 percent. Radically lower prices did not appreciably cut the aggregate crop acreage remaining in use.

Another feature of the 1996 policy—elimination of price supports—has had the effect of sustaining the persistence of low prices. Current US agricultural policy is left with nothing to limit the downward price spiral. Even successive yearly reductions in grain stocks have not had the expected price-enhancing impacts of yesteryear. In the current environment, market participants know that no supply management programs can be used next year to raise prices. So crop demanders do not bid up prices to secure future grain needs. They rightly expect, with all-out production, prices will be as low or lower next season. Over the last five years, market participants have been more and more comfortable with less and less grain in the granary at the end of the crop year. Hence, prices have fallen much farther than they would have under similar stock conditions before 1996.

Prior to 1996, government commodity payments were generally used as financial incentives to encourage farmers to participate in supply management programs. Since 1996, government commodity payments are strictly income support payments. The Congressional response to the massive price slide was to institute record-level payments to farmers, to partially compensate for lost income. . . . Beginning in 1998, subsidies to farmers increased by 250 percent over the period 1990–1997. Post-1997 subsidies took the form of unanticipated loan deficiency payments (LDPs), marketing loan gains, and ad hoc/emergency/disaster payments.

Low prices triggered high subsidies in the US, not the reverse, as many believe. While some blame high US subsidies for low prices, the data clearly show the opposite: that higher and higher subsidies were authorized in response to lower and lower prices and incomes. The problem is not the income-support payments that were added by recent legislation but the supply control and price-supporting mechanisms that were taken away.

Low prices would not be a problem if demand increased enough to compensate for the lower per-unit price. But this is not the case. Despite record-level government payments, farm income continues to slide downward as farmers receive less and less of their income from the market. Even as prices plummeted—making US commodities more competitive in world markets and giving rise to dumping on world markets below the average cost of production—exports remained flat.

Agriculture Markets Do Not Self-Correct

The 1996 real-time test of free markets in agriculture flopped. Small farms are failing in droves, and those that remain are in severe distress. Under the current legislation—extended in the 2002 Farm Bill with the addition of a new income support program that automates the "emergency" payments when prices are low—the accelerator works but the brakes have been disconnected. The goal of growth in productive capacity remains, but the goal of protecting farm prices and incomes by managing the level of production has been abandoned. While the large government payments to producers may have hindered the adjustment process, it is necessary also to recognize that adjusting to the low prices implies a further drop of at least $10 to $12 billion in annual net farm income. This loss of income would have devastating consequences for rural communities and small farmers.

As seen above, once production increased and prices fell, there were no policy mechanisms in place to limit the downward spiral. The agriculture sector did not self-correct as the framers of this new policy had predicted. Though the ambitious export projections of the mid-1990s did not materialize, agriculture could have been spared if, like other industries, its markets could self-correct. In other words, if the assumption was correct that farmers are more price responsive, then they would cut back production on their own, causing a recovery in prices. But that didn't happen. As seen, the government's response to low prices was to pay out record subsidies to compensate for lost income created by low prices. The cause of the low prices was the elimination of government price support and acreage reduction programs. The farmers were simply cultivating more cropland than the market could handle.

Periodical Bibliography

The following articles have been selected to supplement the diverse views presented in this chapter.

Jagdish Bhagwati and Arvind Panagariya	"Why the Trade Talks Collapsed," *Wall Street Journal*, July 7, 2007.
Economist	"Let Them Eat Cake," May 22, 2008.
Timothy Egan	"Red State Welfare," *New York Times*, June 28, 2007.
Lauren Etter and Greg Hitt	"Farm Lobby Beats Back Assault on Subsidies," *Wall Street Journal*, March 27, 2008.
Gazette	"It's Raining Money: There's Never a Drought of Farm Subsidies," July 22, 2006.
Julio Godoy	"Europe: Subsidies Feed Food Scarcity," *Inter Press Service*, April 25, 2008.
Michael Grunwald	"Why Our Farm Policy Is Failing," *Time*, November 12, 2007.
La Crosse Tribune	"Why Do Millionaires Get Federal Farm Subsidies?" December 8, 2008.
Daniella Markheim and Brian M. Riedl	"Farm Subsidies, Free Trade, and the Doha Round," Heritage Foundation WebMemo #1337, February 5, 2007, www.heritage.org.
William McKenzie	"How Subsidies Look from the Family Farm: Some Are Needed, but House Income Limits Fell Short," *Dallas Morning News*, July 31, 2007.
Roy Roberson	"Food, Farming Essential to U.S. Financial Recovery," *Southwest Farm Press*, January 23, 2009.

CHAPTER 2

What Are Some Concerns About Agricultural Subsidies?

Chapter Preface

If global trade were not as widespread as it is currently, there would be little need to consider the impact of a nation's agricultural policy abroad. For example, if global trade was minimal and Japan decided to help its rice farmers survive difficult years, maintain supply, improve quality, and maintain cultural tradition by supporting them with various domestic agricultural subsidies, the impact of such subsidies would likely not be felt outside of Japan. However, in today's global trade environment, when one nation subsidizes its products and those products then are sold in the global market, effects are felt in other nations. For example, if the United States gives its cotton farmers subsidies while a cotton farmer in Mali receives no support, the United States cotton farmer is able to sell his or her product for less than the actual costs of production, whereas the cotton farmer in Mali has to recoup all costs of production without any help from subsidies. Thus, many of the current concerns about agricultural subsidies have to do with the global effects.

One of the major concerns about agricultural subsidies is the effect on developing countries. Wealthy, developed countries spend large amounts of money on domestic and export subsidies, helping their farmers to make a better living and secure a bigger share of the global export market. According to the Congressional Budget Office, domestic agricultural subsidies around the world total over $200 billion a year. Domestic subsidies in the United States and the European Union each account for one-third of the global total, and the countries with the highest rates of subsidies to output include Iceland, Norway, Switzerland, Japan, the United States, and the European Union, all wealthy nations. Meanwhile, developing countries in Africa, Asia, and South America spend little money on domestic subsidies.

Critics such as Thilo Bode, director of the German organization Food Watch, claim that the amount of agricultural subsidies lavished on farmers in rich countries results in unemployment and poverty among farmers in the developing world, and that, in turn, leads to food scarcity, as reported by Julio Godoy in an April 25, 2008, *Inter Press Service* article. Others claim that the lowered prices created by subsidies actually help people in developing countries by making cheap food available for import. In this chapter, the authors debate both the domestic and international effects of agricultural subsidies.

> "Any subsidy that promotes over-
> production and increases exports onto
> the world market at prices below the
> costs of production encourages dump-
> ing."

Agricultural Subsidies Cause Dumping in Developing Countries

Claire Godfrey

*In the following viewpoint, Claire Godfrey argues that agricul-
tural subsidies in the European Union and United States contribute to export dumping, whereby wealthier countries export
agricultural products to developing countries at prices below the
costs of production. Godfrey claims that the high subsidies in
wealthy countries cause the extremely low prices on key commodities, ultimately harming farmers in the developing world.
Claire Godfrey is trade policy advisor for Oxfam International, a
confederation of organizations working to end poverty and injustice.*

As you read, consider the following questions:

1. According to a World Bank study, European Union (EU) subsidies for sugar have caused world market prices to fall by what percentage?

2. According to research performed by Oxfam, export prices of wheat, powdered milk, and sugar from the European Union are fixed at what respective percentages of their production costs?

3. Are agricultural subsidies in the European Union and United States increasing or declining, according to the author?

Jamaica is but one example of where Europe's agricultural subsidies continue to inflict enormous damage on developing countries. Thousands of agricultural producers across the world sell their goods on local, regional, and world markets. Yet many smallholder producers in developing countries suffer low prices, lost market shares, and unfair competition. In Oxfam's experience, the Common Agricultural Policy (CAP) depresses and destabilises markets for non-subsidising exporters, including those in the developing world. The continued practice of dumping—exporting at prices far below the costs of production—is destroying domestic markets in developing countries. This paper shows the impact of dumping EU sugar and dairy products on the livelihoods of farmers in Mozambique, India, and Jamaica. . . .

The beneficiaries of agricultural subsidies are clearly recognised by European policy-makers. But the millions who bear the brunt of the impact of these subsidies are dispersed, hidden, and ignored. Oxfam is working with small farmers around the world and is concerned that their efforts to develop sustainable livelihoods are being undermined by EU agricultural policies. From Mozambique to India to Jamaica, poor farmers are being denied the opportunity to work their way out of poverty.

Sugar Dumping

The EU sugar regime provides one of the most powerful and unambiguous examples of dumping. Mozambique is one of the countries affected—and one of the world's poorest nations. Approximately 80 per cent of its people live in rural areas, where agriculture is almost the only source of employment. Sugar is a high-potential export crop, facilitating livelihood diversification and stabilising household incomes. Production costs are less than ¤286 per tonne, making the country one of the world's most efficient producers. The sugar sector is Mozambique's single largest source of employment, employing 23,000 workers in 2001. If more sugar mills were to be successfully rehabilitated, the number of jobs available could rise to 40,000.

However, the country faces many obstacles in its attempts to rehabilitate production. The dumping of European surpluses reduces Mozambique's export revenues. Despite the EU being one of the highest-cost sugar producers, its subsidies mean that it is the second largest sugar exporter in the world. The EU therefore has a strong influence on world prices. A World Bank study estimates that the EU sugar regime has caused world market prices to fall by 17 per cent. Moreover, Mozambique cannot compete in third markets against cheap, subsidised European sugar. In 2001 for example, Europe exported 770,000 tonnes of white sugar to Algeria and 150,000 tonnes to Nigeria—countries that would be natural export markets for competitive African exporters such as Mozambique. The costs in terms of income and development opportunities are huge. . . .

Dairy Dumping

A major barrier facing India's dairy co-operatives in their quest to expand into new international markets is the flood of heavily subsidised EU dairy products on the global market. Last year [2001] India became the world's largest dairy producer, producing 84 million tonnes of milk. The sector includes a network of co-operatives serving more than 10 million farmers in over 80,000 villages. It has become an immensely valuable industry in a country that is home to one-third of the world's poor.

The EU, the World Bank, UN World Food Programme (WFP), and UN Food and Agriculture Organisation (FAO) have all played a critical role in Operation Flood, the world's largest dairy development programme, which has benefited millions of small dairy farmers all over India. More than ¤2.2bn of financial support has been ploughed into the sector over the last three decades.

The industry is now seeking to expand into new net dairy-importing markets in countries in South-East Asia, the Gulf, and the southern Mediterranean. However, its efforts are being hampered by unfair competition from subsidised European dairy exports. This year [2002], the FAO cites the EU as offering export subsidies at 60 per cent of the international price for whole milk powder, and 136 per cent of the international price for butter.

Dairy dumping also has a serious impact on Jamaica's domestic market. Subsidised European milk powder is replacing locally produced milk as the input for the Jamaican dairy industry. Many local dairy farmers have had to abandon production because most local processors use the cheaper imported milk powder instead. Until the early 1990s, Jamaican farmers were largely protected from these subsidised imports and the sector was doing well. But when the government was forced to liberalise imports as part of World Bank–led adjustment policies, dairy farmers began to suffer. While hundreds of thousands of dollars of aid have been spent on supporting the development of Jamaica's dairy farming, EU export subsidies are undermining these efforts.

In a fair trading system, developing countries would have access to measures that give them greater flexibility to protect their smallholder farmers from surges of cheap or unfairly subsidised imports. However, unless the EU stops using more than ¤1.7bn in annual export subsidies on dairy products, the future of dairy farming in countries such as Jamaica looks bleak indeed.

The Beneficiaries of Subsidies

In 2001, France was again recorded as the main recipient of CAP funding, claiming 22.2 per cent of the total budget of ¤41.53bn. The next biggest recipients were Spain (14.8 per cent), Germany (14.1 per cent), and Italy (12.8 per cent). Some member states and the agribusiness lobby frequently stress the vulnerability of small farmers as an argument for maintaining agricultural policies as they are. Without these safety nets, they argue, the market would destroy those who sustain our rural areas, which would contradict the wishes of European citizens. But in practice, the main beneficiaries of farm support measures are the largest farmers and agribusinesses.

In a detailed breakdown of aid payments across the EU in 2000, the EC [European Commission] calculated that 78 per cent of EU farmers receive less than ¤5000 per year in direct aid. Furthermore, fewer than 2000 of Europe's 4.5 million farmers between them rake in almost ¤1bn in direct aid from the CAP. Farm subsidies also vary in scale across Europe. In Portugal, approximately 95 per cent of farmers receive less than the ¤5000 each year, compared with 43 per cent in the UK. Moreover, 380 of the UK's landowners and large-scale agricultural businesses glean aid in excess of the ¤300,000 per farmer ceiling on annual payments proposed in the mid-term review.

By concentrating subsidies in the hands of its richest agricultural landowners, EU agricultural policies are hastening the demise of smallholder agriculture in Europe. In most countries where rural land accounts for the majority of their territory, such as Spain, Italy, and Greece, the active rural population has been reduced to one-fifth of its number in the 1950s. Large-scale corporate agriculture and the powerful lobbies of the largest European farmers have successfully influenced the direction and content of the CAP from its inception. They continue to defend it against reform, as they reap substantial profits from aid systems such as export subsidies.

The real challenge that EU member states are failing to address is that of supporting farm incomes at far lower levels of production. In this respect, much more should be done to link income support to less industrial and more environmentally sensitive systems of production. At the same time, the regressive character of CAP support, with the largest farms and agro-processing companies receiving the lion's share of transfers, should be changed.

The Incentive to Generate Surpluses

The CAP was developed in the early 1960s largely around a price support mechanism and protected borders. By providing incentives to producers, it aimed to avoid food shortages by developing a stable internal food market on the basis of a high level of self-sufficiency. Twenty years later, oversupply in European markets became unavoidable, and excess production found an outlet on international markets. Since the CAP reforms of 1992, the EU has continued to pursue a strategy of agricultural competitiveness in international markets by a combination of export subsidies, internal price support, and direct aid to producers to compensate for revenue losses.

Today, the EU accounts for 18 per cent of world sugar exports, 28 percent of world dairy exports, and around 8 per cent (and rising fast) of world wheat exports. Despite production costs, with rare exceptions, being considerably higher in Europe than in many other countries, the EU has maintained its large market share through the CAP's complex range of subsidies. Subsidies support production and generate sur-

Farming in the Developing World

More than three-quarters of the poor in the developing world—some 900 million people—live in rural areas. Most are small farmers. That is why agricultural growth based on smallholder producers is one of the most powerful catalysts for poverty reduction: for every additional $1 generated through agricultural production, economic linkages can add another $3 to the rural economy. Support to agriculture in rich countries matters because it restricts opportunities for the pro-poor rural growth that northern governments like to endorse at international meetings. And it matters because the rural poor cannot wait any longer for meaningful reform.

There is a cruel irony at the heart of the current agricultural trading system. In rich countries, agriculture represents a small share of national income and employment, typically less than 2 percent of the total. By contrast, agriculture accounts for 17 percent of gross domestic product (GDP) in middle-income countries, rising to 35 percent in the poorest countries. Agricultural exports exceed one-third of the total in almost half of all developing countries. Yet industrialized countries systematically use subsidies to skew the benefits of agricultural trade in their favor.

Kevin Watkins and Joachim von Braun,
"Time to Stop Dumping on the World's Poor,"
International Food Policy Research Institute, 2003,
www.ifpri.org.

pluses of many products, such as sugar, dairy, and wheat. This surplus is then exported outside the EU at prices below the cost of production. Oxfam's research shows that export prices of wheat, powdered milk, and sugar are fixed at 34 per cent, 50 per cent, and 75 per cent respectively of their production costs.

Subsidised European agricultural exports not only undermine the livelihoods of smallholder farmers in developing countries, but are also a huge cost to taxpayers, consumers, and the environment. In 2002, the CAP will cost a massive ¤46.5bn—almost half the EU budget. Farm subsidies will account for 37 per cent of the total value of European agricultural production. In a recent survey by the European opinion research service, Eurobarometer, Europeans expressed strong support (more than 70 per cent) for those aspects of the CAP relating to food quality, protection of the environment, and improvement in the quality of life in rural areas (known as the multi-functionality of agriculture). However, when asked whether they believed that the current CAP fulfilled these functions efficiently, only three out of every ten people surveyed replied positively.

EU domestic support should be restructured towards less industrial agriculture and measures to enhance the welfare of small farmers rather than large-scale corporate agriculture, without undermining food security and rural livelihoods in developing countries.

The Subsidies That Encourage Dumping

Any subsidy that promotes over-production and increases exports onto the world market at prices below the costs of production encourages dumping. Under the WTO Agreement on Agriculture, developed countries made a commitment to reduce their agricultural subsidies. In practice, they have done the opposite. EU agricultural subsidies were approximately $5bn higher at the end of the 1990s than a decade earlier. The US is no better, having just adopted a Farm Bill which is estimated will increase agricultural subsidies over the next decade by 80 per cent to a total of at least $US82bn.

Market-price support and farm payments linked to output are the major form of producer support in rich countries, accounting for almost three-quarters of payments in 2000. These programmes tend to operate in a similar way. Governments buy agricultural commodities at prices above world market levels, transferring income to their farmers. They then transfer the same commodities onto world markets, usually with the help of hefty subsidies, thus pushing down world prices.

Arguments in favour of the immediate elimination of export subsidies are compelling. Despite this, the EU still accounts for 90 per cent of the world's export subsidies. It is true that between 1990 and 1999 export subsidies fell from 31 per cent to 14 per cent of CAP expenditure. However, these figures tell only part of the story. Over the same period, CAP spending rose from ¤24.9bn to ¤39.5bn. As a result, export subsidies fell by less than one-third, and not by the 55 per cent implied.

According to the EU, the overall level of support to agriculture matters less than the structure of subsidies. The EU contends that it has scaled down subsidies that directly encourage production in favour of direct payments to farmers and payments not linked to production (or 'decoupling' of payments). In theory, the further decoupling of subsidies linked to production, increased conditionality with regard to environmental, animal welfare, and food safety standards, and a further shift to investment in rural development proposed in the EC's mid-term review are intended to discourage overproduction still further. While this proposal is welcome, in practice it may not have this effect.

The OECD [Organization for Economic Co-operation and Development] has noted that even 'de-coupled' payments influence decisions about production, because they send a strong signal to farmers that they can expect to receive extra support when world prices are low. This affects the international competitiveness of EU and US agricultural production, and the price at which these countries are able to export onto world markets. The real challenge is for the EU to support farm incomes at far lower levels of production by developing market regulatory systems that stabilise prices and provide a predictable environment for producers.

The cereals sector provides a good illustration of the negative effects of direct payments. In 1992 the EU shifted to a system of direct payments that no longer depended on export subsidies. Since then EU cereal prices have fallen by around half but production has risen; exports are rising to pre-reform levels. The OECD predicts that the decline in EU wheat prices, together with a sustained increase in the world price, will improve EU competitiveness on the world market, and that EU wheat exports will increase significantly in the next ten years. If current policies remain unchanged, the EU's share of world wheat markets will increase from its current level of 7.85 per cent to 19.7 per cent in 2012, leading to efficient producers in areas such as southern Africa seeing their market share further squeezed.

This is not to argue against the use of carefully targeted policies in the EU that promote legitimate rural development and environmental objectives. But the idea that existing industrialised-country agricultural policies are good for rural development and the environment is a myth. On the contrary, current subsidy patterns, with their emphasis on expanding production, have encouraged the industrialisation of agriculture, with a premium on the heavy use of chemical inputs. The most immediate consequences include extensive environmental damage and threats to public health. Moreover, the EU's own figures show that rural development played a minor role (only 10.5 per cent) in farm spending in most countries, Austria and Finland together taking 83 per cent of that amount.

End Dumping

EU leaders must take urgent action to end dumping, which is so damaging to smallholder farmers in developing countries.

Oxfam recognises that an end to dumping will generate adjustment costs in Europe. Policy makers in Europe have responsibilities for rural development and the environment. But as representatives of one of the world's richest and most powerful trading blocs, they also have responsibilities towards developing countries. Reforming a system that reaps big rewards for a minority in Europe, while undermining the markets and opportunities for farmers and agricultural labourers in the developing world, is an essential step towards making trade fair and making globalisation work for the poor.

> "U.S. farm subsidies are frequently
> blamed for agricultural dumping, yet
> they are only a symptom of a much
> deeper market failure."

Agricultural Subsidies Are Not the Cause of Dumping in Developing Countries

Sophia Murphy, Ben Lilliston, and Mary Beth Lake

In the following viewpoint, Sophia Murphy, Ben Lilliston, and Mary Beth Lake argue that agricultural dumping is not the result of agricultural subsidies but, rather, a result of the elimination of supply management programs. Without supply management policies, the authors argue, small farmers around the globe have suffered. Sophia Murphy is senior advisor and Ben Lilliston is communications director at the Institute for Agriculture and Trade Policy, and Mary Beth (Lake) Graebert is associate director of operations at the Land Policy Institute.

As you read, consider the following questions:

1. According to the authors, wheat, soybeans, corn, cotton, and rice were exported from the United States in 2003 at what respective percentages below the cost of production?

2. What occurred in 1996, according to the authors, that led to increases in agricultural dumping?

3. According to the authors, without a supply management strategy, the elimination of agricultural subsidies will have what effect on U.S. agriculture?

January 1, 2005 marked the 10-year anniversary of the World Trade Organization's [WTO's] Agreement on Agriculture (AoA). When governments launched the agreement, they hailed it as a victory for farmers around the world: farmers were to benefit from more trade, greater access to markets and higher prices. A decade later, there is unquestionably more trade in agricultural products. However, higher and fair prices for farmers seem further away than ever. It is hard to make the case that the Agreement on Agriculture has done anything to benefit farmers anywhere in the world.

Since the WTO's inception, widespread agricultural dumping—the selling of products at below their cost of production—by global agri-business companies based in the United States and European Union has wreaked havoc on global agricultural markets. Hit the hardest are farmers in poor countries who are often pushed off the farm by dumped agricultural commodities.

An examination of U.S. government data indicates that since the WTO began, U.S.-based companies have engaged in steady, high levels of agricultural dumping in their global sales of the five most exported commodities. While global food companies have greatly benefited from the low prices for the raw materials of their products, farmers around the world, including U.S. farmers, are going out of business.

Rampant Dumping Continues

The Institute for Agriculture and Trade Policy (IATP) has documented export dumping from U.S.-based multinational corporations onto world agricultural markets for the last 14 years. The U.S. is one of the world's largest sources of dumped agricultural commodities. This analysis is based on the most recent numbers available—2003. It updates IATP's more comprehensive dumping report issued in 2001. This analysis provides dumping calculations from 1990 to 2003 for five commodities grown in the U.S. and sold on the world market: wheat, corn (maize), soybeans, rice and cotton.

Data from the U.S. Department of Agriculture (USDA) and the Organization for Economic Cooperation and Development (OECD) are used to compare the cost of production, including producer input costs paid by the government (a portion of the subsidies calculated in the OECD's producer support estimate, or PSE) with the export price. . . .

The latest numbers available show a continued trend of widespread agricultural dumping from U.S.-based global food and agribusiness companies. In 2003, agriculture exports continued to be sold well below the cost of production:

- *Wheat* was exported at an average price of 28 percent below cost of production.

- *Soybeans* were exported at an average price of 10 percent below cost of production.

- *Corn* was exported at an average price of 10 percent below cost of production.

- *Cotton* was exported at an average price of 47 percent below cost of production.

- *Rice* was exported at an average price of 26 percent below cost of production. . . .

The 2003 data indicated an across the board decrease in levels of dumping from the previous year for all five commodities. However, this decrease is widely recognized to be the result of reduced supply, caused by bad weather and pest infestation, [which] bumped up prices. The decrease was not the result of any changes in international trade rules or domestic farm programs. The 2003 levels of dumping are very consistent with the trend of high levels of dumping for all five commodities since the WTO's inception in 1995. Ominously, U.S. commodity prices for several crops, particularly corn, have plunged in 2004, suggesting dumping levels will increase again when final numbers are available for 2004.

The Harmful Effects of Dumping

Dumping is one of the most damaging of all current distortions in world trade. Developing country agriculture, vital for food security, rural livelihoods, poverty reduction and generating foreign exchange, is crippled by the competition from major commodities sold at well below cost of production prices in world markets.

The structural price depression associated with agricultural dumping has two major effects on developing country farmers who raise competing products. First, below-cost imports drive developing country farmers out of their local markets. If the farmers do not have access to a safety net of subsidies and credit, they have to abandon their land. When this happens, the farm economy shrinks, in turn shrinking the rural economy as a whole and sending rural people into trade-related migration. Second, developing country farmers who sell their products to exporters find their global market share undermined by the policy of a depressed "global price." The cascading effects of dumping are felt around the world in places as far apart as Jamaica, Burkina Faso and the Philippines.

The 2003 dumping numbers also illustrate the disastrous impact of U.S. agricultural policy on U.S. farmers, who face prices well below their cost of production for these five major crops. While the U.S. government has put in place support programs to make up some of the income farmers lose from low prices, it is seldom enough. Larger, corporate farms receive the bulk of subsidy payments. From 1997 to 2002, the U.S. lost over 90,000 farms of below 2,000 acres, while 3,600 farms grew to more than 2,000 acres, according to the U.S. Department of Agriculture. And despite the high levels of dumping, U.S. agricultural exports have not gained market share around the world. In fact, U.S. agricultural exports lost value between 1995 ($80 billion) to 2003 ($76 billion) and the U.S. share of the world agriculture export market declined from 14 percent in 1990 to 11.3 percent in 2003. . . . Additionally, most experts, including the USDA, project that the U.S. will become a net agricultural importer sometime in 2005. Allowing sales of agricultural products at prices that do not touch actual production costs to go on for almost a decade is no way to do business.

U.S. Farm Bills and Dumping

Dumping by U.S.-based corporations is possible because commodity production is badly managed. The 1996 and 2002 U.S. Farm Bills have produced a vast structural, price-depressing oversupply of most major agricultural commodities. This oversupply has driven prices down. Both the 1996 and 2002 Farm Bills were driven by efforts to make them compliant with WTO rules. The result has been the institutionalization of agricultural dumping by U.S. farm policy.

U.S. farm subsidies are frequently blamed for agricultural dumping, yet they are only a symptom of a much deeper market failure. The sharp increases in agricultural dumping in the U.S. can be traced to the 1996 U.S. Farm Bill, which stripped away already weakened programs that were designed

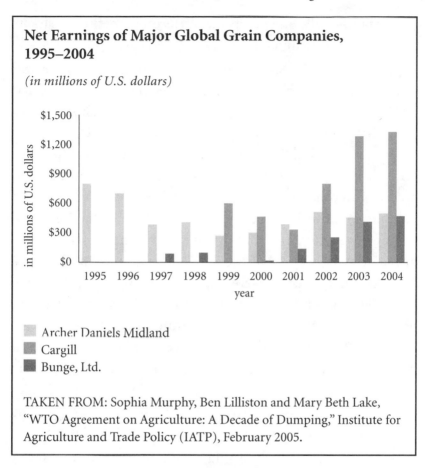

Net Earnings of Major Global Grain Companies, 1995–2004

(in millions of U.S. dollars)

Archer Daniels Midland
Cargill
Bunge, Ltd.

TAKEN FROM: Sophia Murphy, Ben Lilliston and Mary Beth Lake, "WTO Agreement on Agriculture: A Decade of Dumping," Institute for Agriculture and Trade Policy (IATP), February 2005.

to manage supply. These supply management programs helped to balance supply with demand, ensuring a fair return to farmers from the marketplace. They cost the taxpayer relatively little. The pre-1996 commodity programs in effect set a floor price that commodity buyers had to pay farmers. The programs helped to correct a structural flaw in agricultural markets: with millions of producers and only a handful of processors, commodity markets do not function according to the textbook theories of sellers and buyers having equal supply/demand information and negotiating power at the moment of sale. Given this structural imbalance in market power between farmers and agribusiness corporations, the government traditionally intervened to ensure competitive markets and prevent anti-competitive business practices.

In 1996, the U.S. government abandoned intervention mechanisms at the behest of agribusiness lobbyists, supported by "free" trade economists. The result: U.S. agricultural prices went into freefall. Without the supply control programs and other interventions, commodity buyers were able to drive prices below the costs of production and leave them there. To prevent the collapse of U.S. agriculture, Congress then set up "counter-cyclical payments" to make up part of the losses resulting from the Farm Bill "reforms." Counter-cyclical payments adopted as part of the 2002 Farm Bill, mask the price "signals" that farmers were supposed to be using to make their planting and livestock investment decisions. The U.S. now has very expensive farm programs that distort market signals while doing nothing to correct the deeper distortion inherent in the unbalanced market power between farmers and commodity buyers and processors. The system is a mess.

The influence of the 1996 Farm Bill on dumping is significant. Each of the five major export commodities saw a significant jump in export dumping when comparing the seven years (1990–1996) prior to the 1996 Farm Bill to the subsequent seven years (1997–2003):

- *Wheat* dumping levels increased from an average of 27 percent per year pre-1996 Farm Bill to 37 percent per year post-1996 Farm Bill.

- *Soybean* dumping levels increased from an average of 2 percent per year pre-1996 Farm Bill to 11.8 percent post-1996 Farm Bill.

- *Maize* dumping levels increased from an average of 6.8 percent per year pre-1996 Farm Bill to 19.2 percent post-1996 Farm Bill.

- *Cotton* dumping levels increased from an average of 29.4 percent pre-1996 Farm Bill to an average of 48.4 percent post-1996 Farm Bill.

- *Rice* dumping levels increased from an average of 13.5 percent pre-1996 Farm Bill to an average of 19.2 percent post-1996 Farm Bill.

The Effect of Subsidies on Dumping

Research by the Agricultural Policy Analysis Center (APAC) at the University of Tennessee, Knoxville concludes that even the total elimination of U.S. farm subsidies, would result in only negligible increases in U.S. prices for corn, wheat and soybeans. The small price increase would then gradually decline to nothing over nine years, as the price rise encouraged new production, oversupply and a resulting price depression. And while there would be more sustained, modest increases in prices for cotton and rice, those increases would not be enough to cover the cost of production, so dumping would continue. APAC concludes that to raise prices structurally for these commodities, some form of supply management is required.

Without supply management policies, farmers (and, increasingly, the farm corporations that are taking over production) will over-produce whether or not they have access to subsidies. The elimination of subsidies, in the absence of a supply management strategy, will simply move the U.S. agricultural landscape even further away from small, diversified family farms toward larger, corporate farms. The total amount of farmland in production will remain largely unchanged.

There is little question that the largest commodity traders, who are now dominant in financing trades, processing and shipping, are the biggest beneficiaries of agricultural dumping. These vertically integrated companies buy their raw material—agricultural commodities—at extremely cheap prices. They control the value-added stages of production and so are sure of a significant profit from the final sales. Nearly all of these companies have seen their profits skyrocket in recent years.

Eliminating Agricultural Dumping

Article Six of the General Agreement on Tariffs and Trade (GATT), which is one of the agreements overseen by the WTO, sets rules that prohibit dumping. However, the rules make it complicated for smaller, poorer countries to establish grounds for anti-dumping duties because of the requirements to demonstrate harm to the sector involved.

Underlying the technical challenges that inhibit the use of WTO rules to discipline dumping is the political reality of the multilateral trading system. When the ultimate threat against dumping is to impose prohibitive tariffs, the tool is a lot easier for a big country such as the U.S. to use than for a small country like Bangladesh. Just under half of Bangladesh's exports are destined for the U.S.; this isn't a trade relationship Bangladesh can afford to jeopardize.

Governments need to make it easier for poor countries to challenge agricultural dumping. The easiest and most WTO-legal approach is for the importing country to have the ability to immediately impose countervailing and anti-dumping duties to bring the dumped prices up to cost of production levels.

However, with the WTO deadlocked over agricultural negotiations and the major powers refusing to tackle this form of trade distortion, it may be time to turn to other international institutions to address dumping. In June 2004, the United Nations Committee on Trade and Development (UNCTAD) met in São Paulo, Brazil and established an international commodity task force to look at, among other issues, agricultural dumping. UNCTAD has historically focused directly on promoting development through trade and has been home to global commodity agreements that have attempted to address chronic oversupply—such as the International Coffee Agreement. In the face of another year of high dumping levels, some governments are showing renewed interest in cooperative, multilateral approaches to better regulate commodity markets.

In addition, the U.S. Congress and the European Commission need to radically restructure their farm programs. Decoupled payments are a failure. Rather than doling out production and income support that goes overwhelmingly to the largest farmers, the European Commission and U.S. Congress should focus agricultural reforms on controlling overproduction and redressing the gross disparity in market power between millions of producers and the three to six firms per commodity that dominate the trade, processing and shipments of agricultural commodities.

A Supply Side Problem

These latest numbers on agricultural dumping by U.S. agribusiness once again illustrate the need for immediate action at the international level. First steps include:

1. The elimination of visible export subsidies, as well as the establishment of strong disciplines on export credits and program food aid, as quickly as possible.

2. A commitment from exporting countries to keep products priced below the cost of production out of world markets.

3. The publication of annual full-cost of production estimates for OECD countries. To fully address agricultural dumping, governments must develop a more thorough and transparent methodology to measure the problem and make the relevant data publicly available within six months of the close of the fiscal year.

4. Agreement on strong international rules to prohibit restrictive business practices among the oligopolies that dominate trade in most agricultural commodities.

In the longer term, governments must again turn their attention to the need for global commodity agreements that manage the supply-side problems. When global oversupply drives prices down for farmers around the world, global commodity agreements have restored the critical balance between supply and demand that has been damaged by the "race to the bottom" results of free trade. When supply and demand are out of balance in agriculture, the consequences are serious. When there is not enough supply, people suffer or go hungry. When there is too much supply, prices drop, farmers suffer and many go out of business. For the vast majority of farmers in the world, that means they, too, go hungry. Modern trade agreements that enable countries to restore the balancing mechanisms for supply and demand would help the world's farmers, while respecting the needs of consumers, particularly the human right to adequate, appropriate and nutritious food.

Developing countries need healthy agricultural sectors to increase food security and rural employment and to decrease poverty. To achieve this, agricultural commodities must be priced fairly. Dumping is a gross distortion of commodity markets. It undermines the livelihoods of 70 percent of the world's poorest people. Trade rules provide the tools needed to address agricultural dumping. These rules should be strengthened, implemented and enforced.

> *"The agricultural trade and subsidy policies in the United States, European Union and Japan . . . are harming poor people in developing countries and making rural development difficult."*

Agricultural Subsidies Harm the Poor in Developing Countries

Per Pinstrup-Andersen

In the following viewpoint, Per Pinstrup-Andersen argues that agricultural subsidies in rich countries are harming poor people in the developing world. Through these subsidies and associated failed attempts to counteract their ill effects, the author contends that farmers in the developing world are unfairly losing market share for their goods, which their communities so desperately need. Per Pinstrup-Andersen is the H.E. Babcock Professor of Food, Nutrition, and Public Policy; the J. Thomas Clark Professor of Entrepreneurship; and professor of applied economics at Cornell University.

As you read, consider the following questions:

1. According to the author, how does the amount of annual subsidy payments to farmers in rich countries compare to the amount of annual development assistance to developing countries?

2. What is the major problem with the Everything But Arms (EBA) program designed by the European Union, according to Pinstrup-Andersen?

3. Which countries does the author believe will be the winners from trade liberalization, and which does he think will have the least to gain?

Strengthening rural communities in low-income countries is extremely important to reduce poverty, hunger and related human misery. Three out of every four poor people live in rural areas and most of them depend on agriculture for their meager incomes, either as farmers with smallholdings, farm workers, or providers of goods and services purchased by farmers.

The Multiplier Effect

If farmers do not make money, neither does anybody else in rural communities. On the other hand, when farmers do make money, they spend it on things that generate employment and income throughout the economy. The economy grows and people in both rural and urban areas escape poverty. This so-called "multiplier effect" is much stronger in small-scale agriculture than in any other sector of a low-income country. There is no better illustration of the "multiplier effect" than the developments in China during the 1980s. While most countries are struggling to reach the Millennium Development Goals for poverty and hunger alleviation by 2015, China has already achieved them.

Towards the end of the 1970s, the Chinese government introduced a new set of policies that effectively gave Chinese farmers an opportunity to make more money. The opportunities were well received by the farmers, who increased their purchase of fertilizers, pesticides, and consumer goods such as bicycles, radios and a large number of other goods and services. Construction boomed in rural areas and employment and incomes rose rapidly in both rural and urban areas, resulting in the beginning of a long period of high economic growth and rapid reduction in poverty and hunger.

There are other success stories to show the importance of agricultural growth in alleviating poverty and hunger, including the impact of the Green Revolution in Indonesia, Korea, Taiwan and India to mention a few. Unfortunately, agricultural growth is limited in most low-income countries and, partly as a consequence, very little if any reduction in poverty and hunger is occurring.

Policies of Harm

The agricultural trade and subsidy policies in the United States, European Union and Japan (hereafter called "the rich countries") are harming poor people in developing countries and making rural development difficult. The harm done by far exceeds the good done by development assistance.

A few numbers may illustrate the problem. The annual subsidy payment received by farmers in rich countries is about $280 billion. The total annual development assistance to developing countries is about $60 billion, or less than one quarter of the subsidies. A Japanese dairy cow receives about $3,000 in annual subsidy, and the dairy cow in the EU gets about $1,000. In comparison, the average annual income of citizens in Sub-Saharan Africa is about $500, and the development assistance from the EU and Japan to sub-Saharan Africa is about $10 per African.

If developing country farmers, who do not receive subsidies, cannot sell their products at a price above production costs, they cannot earn the incomes needed to escape poverty and they cannot generate the aforementioned multiplier effect that would help others out of poverty. The net result is continuation of poverty, hunger and related misery.

These policies are taking markets away from poor farmers, not because poor farmers are inefficient but because they cannot compete with highly subsidized farmers in rich countries who can sell below production costs. High import tariffs also keep low-cost developing country farmers out of rich countries' markets. Import tariffs on products that developing country farmers can produce cheaper than rich country farmers such as rice, sugar and cotton are high precisely to keep poor farmers out of the markets and protect high prices within the rich countries. Import tariffs and subsidized export of what cannot be sold in the rich country markets are the tools for maintaining these high domestic prices. The rich country consumers pay and poor country farmers are not given a chance.

Whether the consumer or the taxpayer pays, the consequences for poor countries and poor people within are severe. They depend directly or indirectly on agriculture. If they are unable to sell what they produce, they make no money and they continue to suffer from poverty and hunger, their children continue to be malnourished and many die.

The Reasons for the Policies

So, why do such policies continue to exist? Partly because a small but politically powerful minority of the population in rich countries—the land owners—and agribusinesses would lose if the policies were changed, and partly because inertia in the policy process makes it difficult to change policies that in fact served a legitimate purpose when they were first introduced many years ago. Another reason is that rich

The Importance of Agriculture

Historically, agriculture has been a major pillar—if not the foundation—of developing economies because it provides food security, creates employment and generates local capital. For example, in 1790, nearly 90 percent of the U.S. workforce was employed in agriculture. By 1900, farmers dropped to 38 percent of the labor force, and today they account for less than 1 percent. Agriculture accounts for less than 1 percent of U.S. gross domestic product (GDP). Similar trends in other OECD [Organization for Economic Cooperation and Development] countries indicate that the path to development begins with agriculture.

Max Borders and H. Sterling Burnett,
"Farm Subsidies: Devastating the
World's Poor and the Environment,"
National Center for Policy and Analysis,
March 24, 2006, www.ncpa.org.

societies wish to ensure that farmers have a reasonable income level relative to others in the society.

All of these reasons could be dealt with in a manner that would not penalize poor people. Landowners could be compensated for falling land prices, agribusiness could adjust to new opportunities, voters and politicians could be informed that the original purposes are no longer valid, and farmers could be paid an income supplement that would not require import tariffs and surplus production.

Failed Solutions

In an effort to help the 49 least developed countries, the EU designed a program called Everything But Arms (EBA), which would permit these countries free access to the EU markets without paying tariffs for any products except arms. The major problem with the EBA is a safety clause that permits the EU to close imports of any product if it threatens domestic suppliers. In other words, imports coming from poor farmers in the least developed countries can be stopped if they threaten to be more competitive than what rich-country farmers produce. Is it a surprise that little import has occurred? The main value of the EBA appears to be public relations for the EU on the assumption that no one would be interested in reading the fine print.

The United States has a similar provision that permits selected low-income African countries to export certain commodities into the United States without tariff. As in the case of the EBA, these countries have exported very little through that provision, with the exception of oil, which did not need the provision in the first place.

Preferential treatment given to some developing countries is much more valuable. The EU admits fixed amounts of sugar from selected developing countries without tariff and pays the high internal EU price. The downside of this arrangement is that the imported sugar adds to the sugar surplus that the EU then exports at prices below production costs with the negative impact mentioned above. One of the world's largest sugar exporters, the EU produces sugar at much higher costs than most poor countries.

Likewise, the United States is the world's largest exporter of cotton even though cotton is produced much cheaper by farmers in poor countries. But they do not get a chance. U.S. cotton producers receive very large subsidies. In response, they produce more than can be sold in the United States. The rest is exported at prices below cost of production taking the export opportunities away from farmers in poor countries.

Export of subsidized maize, wheat, rice, oil-seed, dairy products and meat at prices below production costs and dumping of surpluses on poor country markets make life miserable for poor country farmers. But why do poor countries not protect themselves by implementing import tariffs and refuse to accept food at prices below production costs? For one thing, it is likely to be prohibited for countries that are members of the World Trade Organization. Furthermore, many poor countries are net importers of food. An import tariff would be a regressive tax on consumers.

Well-meaning development assistance from rich countries sometimes conflicts with the same countries' agricultural trade policies. EU development assistance to the Dominican Republic was successful in developing a small-scale dairy sector, helping poor farmers out of poverty. Unfortunately, soon after this development success, the EU decided to dump some of its surplus of milk powder resulting from EU dairy subsidies. A good bit of the milk powder ended up in the Dominican Republic and was reconstituted and sold at prices below the cost of production in both the EU and the Dominican Republic. The consequences for the Dominican dairy farmers were as could be predicted.

One way to help poor people out of poverty is to generate employment by adding value to agricultural commodities through processing. Development assistance agencies are fully aware of that opportunity and have provided funds for a variety of such activities, often with export in mind. At the same time, rich countries maintain the so-called tariff escalation, which increases the rate of import tariff along with increasing processing. Not exactly an incentive to developing countries to add value to agricultural commodities.

The reason for tariff escalation is clear. Rich countries want to create the employment and added value in their own countries. They want poor countries to export the raw materials such as green coffee in bulk instead of roasted coffee nicely packaged for the retail market. Sounds like a practice left over from colonial times.

Trade Liberalization

Would poor countries really benefit from trade liberalization or would middle-income countries such as Brazil and Thailand reap the benefits? Could poor countries in fact end up losing out because preferential arrangements they now enjoy would be replaced by the removal of tariffs for all?

Countries with good infrastructure and appropriate policies will be the winners from trade liberalization. That means Brazil, Thailand and other middle-income countries and poor people within those countries. Poor countries with poor infrastructure and inappropriate policies are much less likely to gain.

Poor countries should prepare for the day when trade liberalization occurs by investing in roads and other rural infrastructure, appropriate institutions, market development, research to develop appropriate technology for small farmers, and primary health and education for rural areas. But these investments should be made anyway, irrespective of trade considerations. Without them, poverty, hunger, malnutrition and the related human suffering will continue. Rural communities will not be strengthened and the Millennium Development Goals are a mere illusion.

"The common assertion that agricultural liberalization in rich countries would bring large benefits to LDCs [least developed countries] is mistaken."

Agricultural Subsidies Benefit the Least Developed Countries

Arvind Panagariya

In the following viewpoint, Arvind Panagariya argues that it is a mistake to believe that elimination of agricultural subsidies in rich countries will benefit poor countries, particularly the least developed countries. He claims that these countries benefit from the current system of agricultural subsidies because they can sell exports for high prices and buy imports for low prices. Arvind Panagariya is the Jagdish Bhagwati Professor of Indian Political Economy in the Department of International and Public Affairs, and professor of economics at Columbia University. He is author of India: The Emerging Giant.

As you read, consider the following questions:

1. According to Panagariya, what is distinctive about so-called amber box subsidies?

Arvind Panagariya, "Liberalizing Agriculture," *Foreign Affairs*, WTO Special Edition, vol. 84, December 2005, pp. 56–66. Copyright © 2005 by the Council on Foreign Relations, Inc. All rights reserved. Reproduced by permission of Foreign Affairs, www.foreignaffairs.org.

2. In what way does the author think that the numbers commonly cited about subsidies are misleading?

3. What two features do tariffs, export subsidies, and domestic subsidies have in common, according to Panagariya?

Before the Uruguay Round Agreement on Agriculture (URAA) came into effect on January 1, 1995, international trade in agriculture had remained almost entirely outside of the scope of the General Agreement on Tariffs and Trade (GATT). Over the years, powerful farm lobbies in developed countries had sought and received border protections complemented by price supports and export and output subsidies. Developing countries did not object much. Convinced that development was synonymous with industrialization, they focused on seeking access to the developed countries' markets in industrial products.

The Tariff Regime

Given the highly distorted regime that resulted and the continued influence of farm lobbies in economically powerful countries, the URAA was little more than a step in the right direction toward rationalizing, and then dismantling, the inherited protectionist regime. The agreement was implemented in developed countries from 1995 to 2000 and in developing countries from 1995 to 2005. It required each WTO [World Trade Organization] member to replace all border barriers (tariffs, quotas, and combinations of the two) against the imports of agricultural commodities with an equivalent tariff. The replacement tariff was intended to approximate the protectionist effect of existing tariff and nontariff barriers. (This so-called tariffication process was intended to introduce transparency and to rationalize the protectionist regime.) The resulting tariff was then "bound," meaning that it would henceforth define the maximum legal tariff on the commodity.

The URAA required member countries to cut their bound tariffs by a predetermined percentage according to an agreed-upon timetable. But by taking advantage of the high protection in the base period (1986–88) and flexibility in defining a tariff equivalent, virtually all countries managed to bind the tariffs on their import-sensitive commodities at levels substantially higher than the prevailing official tariff, called the Most Favored Nation (MFN) tariff in GATT/WTO terminology. Anticipating that in many cases even the MFN rates were prohibitively high, the URAA required member countries to guarantee a prespecified minimum (de minimis) market access for each product. Most countries chose to meet this requirement by introducing a quota equal to the de minimis obligation and a third, even lower, tariff on imports within the quota. After the quota is filled, the tariff jumps to the MFN rate.

Doha Round negotiations are over the bound rates. Because the bound rate is often substantially higher than the applied rate (which is either the MFN rate or the lower within-quota rate), no actual liberalization will take place in many commodities unless the Doha negotiations bring deep cuts.

The Domestic Subsidy Regime

Although the URAA tariff regime is complicated, the domestic-subsidy regime the agreement has spawned is substantially more so. Under current WTO rules, countries are free to employ four categories of subsidies: those in the "green" and "blue" boxes, certain development measures, and the separate de minimis subsidies. Subsidies in the green box have no or minimal distorting effect on production and hence trade. They include measures decoupled from output such as income-support payments, safety-net programs, payments under environmental programs, and agricultural research-and-development subsidies. The blue box contains direct payments under production-limiting programs. They cover payments based on acreage, yield, or number of livestock in a base year.

Because countries are allowed to revise the base year over time, subsidies in the blue box may have an effect on current output. Development measures cover direct or indirect assistance aimed at encouraging agricultural and rural development in developing countries. They include investment subsidies generally available to agriculture (e.g., research and development, extension programs, and soil and water conservation) and agricultural input subsidies available to low-income or resource-poor farmers (e.g., fertilizer, water, and electricity). Finally, under the de minimis provision, developed countries are allowed to use other subsidies with an aggregate value of up to 5 percent of the total value of domestic agricultural production (developing countries can use them up to 10 percent).

The WTO assigns all subsidies outside of the green and blue boxes and development measures—such as support prices, direct production subsidies, and input subsidies, including those permitted under the de minimis rules—to an "amber" box. These are generally trade-distorting and therefore the proper subject for reduction in the multilateral trade negotiations. Hence, the URAA targeted the Aggregate Measurement of Support (AMS), defined as the amber-box subsidies net of de minimis subsidies. It required member countries to report their total AMS for the period between 1986 and 1988, bind it, and reduce it according to an agreed-upon schedule. Those reductions have now been fully implemented, but there remains a large gap between the bound and the applied AMS.

Subsiding Subsidies

Although export subsidies are very much in the news, they are no longer a major source of trade distortion, at least in aggregate. The URAA required all countries to report, bind, and reduce their export subsidies, as with AMS. Countries reporting no export subsidies on a commodity had to bind the relevant subsidy at zero. Only 25 WTO members, including nine developing countries, reported having any export subsidies, and all of the subsidies applied only to a limited set of commodities. Like tariffs, bound rates for export subsidies are higher than applied rates.

The latest year for which complete data from the WTO on export subsidies are available is 1998. The total amount of export subsidies spent by all WTO members that year was $5.4 billion. The EU accounted for $4.95 billion, followed by Switzerland, with $292 million, and the United States, with $147 million. Because the level of U.S. subsidies dropped to $80 million in 1999 and EU subsidies to $2.6 billion in 2000, it is safe to assume that total export subsidies are currently probably less than $3 billion worldwide and definitely no more than $5 billion. Surprisingly, therefore, the total elimination of export subsidies would be not a big leap but a small step.

Meanwhile, trade-distorting domestic subsidies are much larger than export subsidies, but the reality is less dire than is commonly assumed. Under the URAA, only 34 countries reported AMS subsidies in the base period. Although many developing countries, such as Argentina, Brazil, Mexico, South Korea, South Africa, and Thailand, were in this group, their subsidies were small relative to those in the major developed countries; subsidies are more difficult to finance in poor countries with tighter budget constraints.

Based on the latest and most complete data available from the WTO, total AMS provided by the top five domestic-subsidy users—in order, the EU, the United States, Japan, Switzerland, and Norway—was $71.1 billion in 1998. (The EU's share was $51 billion and that of the United States was $10.4 billion.) Extending the list to the top ten users, thereby also including Mexico, South Korea, Canada, Israel, and Thailand, increases the total to only $74.8 billion. Even including blue-box and de minimis subsidies (permitted under the current WTO rules) yields a total of only $100.7 billion for the top five and $106

> ## Elimination of Agricultural Subsidies
>
> The World Bank has estimated the gains for the developing world if rich countries were to eliminate all of their subsidies, and open all of their markets completely to every export—manufactured as well as agricultural goods—from low and middle-income countries. . . . A lot of countries—most of Latin America, for example—would actually suffer a net loss from the elimination of agricultural subsidies.
>
> *Mark Weisbrot,*
> *"No Boost for Development in World Trade Negotiations,"*
> *Center for Economic and Policy Research, www.cepr.net.*

billion for the top ten (with Brazil replacing Thailand on the latter list). And all indications from the available information are that these numbers are smaller today than they were in 1998. The EU, in particular, has been moving steadily toward turning its amber-box subsidies into green-box subsidies.

Rhetoric and Reality

Yet the numbers commonly cited in the debates about subsidies are far larger. A recent *New York Times* editorial on the Doha Round repeated the often-cited figure that developed countries spend $1 billion per day in agricultural subsidies. [Former] World Bank President Paul Wolfowitz referred to developed countries expending "$280 billion on support to agricultural producers" in a recent op-ed in the *Financial Times*. Oxfam routinely accuses rich countries of giving more than $300 billion annually in subsidies to agribusiness.

The press, nongovernmental organizations (NGOs), and senior staff members at international financial institutions have been either naïve or disingenuous in making these inflated claims. Instead of using estimates of export subsidies and amber-box subsidies (the only subsidies all WTO members consider trade-distorting), they have chosen to focus on an altogether different concept, the Organization for Economic Cooperation and Development's Producer Support Estimates (PSE). It is misleading to call these subsidies: the PSE measures total revenues earned by producers over the world price, whether as a result of tariff protection, export subsidies, output subsidies, or price-support programs. This means that even if there were zero subsidies as conventionally defined but tariffs or quotas raised the domestic price above the world price, the PSE would be positive. Few economists would approve of such a definition of subsidy.

Routine assertions regarding tariffs are also mistaken and misleading. Contrary to complaints by NGOs, media, and international bureaucracies about developed countries' "double standards," developing countries more than match developed-country tariff protection in agriculture. Calculations of trade-weighted average applied tariffs in 2001, the latest year for which data are available, prove the point. At the aggregate level, the rate for such tariffs was 14.3 percent in developed countries and 20.9 percent in developing countries. The rate was 35.5 percent in Japan, 28.6 percent in the European Free Trade Area, 11.8 percent in the EU, and 2.7 percent in the United States. The rate was 93.9 percent in South Korea, 44.1 percent in India, 38.9 percent in China, 30.4 percent in Pakistan, 25.6 percent in those sub-Saharan African states not classed as least-developed countries (LDCs), and 12.9 percent in Mercosur (the South American trading bloc including Argentina, Brazil, Uruguay, and Paraguay).

These aggregate rates mask important variations across commodities. In particular, commodities for which countries had to introduce a quota and a tariff rate lower than their MFN rate under the URAA are subject to disproportionately high tariffs. For example, the trade-weighted average applied tariff on these goods (including, in the United States, certain dairy products, beef, cotton, peanuts, sugar, some products containing sugar, and tobacco) was 36.9 percent in developed and 63.7 percent in developing countries. The rate reached 103 percent in Japan and 226 percent in South Korea. Thus, any liberalization must focus specifically on this set of products.

Sugar is highly protected in virtually all major developed and developing countries. It is subject to the following MFN rates, for example: 72 percent in South Africa, 60 percent in India and Japan, 56 percent in high-income developing Asia, 43 percent in the United States, 23 percent in Central America and the EU (and 74 percent in other European countries), 18 percent in China, and 17 percent in Argentina and Brazil. Thus, reforming tariffs on sugar will require virtually all WTO members to liberalize. The EU and the United States are major offenders, but others—including developing countries— are not without blame.

Although bound tariffs are much higher than applied tariffs worldwide, the gap is much larger in developing countries. In developed countries, the average bound rate is nearly twice as large as the applied rate; in developing countries, it is two and a half times larger. Bangladesh offers the most egregious example: its average bound rate is more than ten times the average applied rate. India, Pakistan, and sub-Saharan Africa also have bound rates more than three times as large as their applied rate. Therefore, unless tariff cuts are deep, and the special treatment that privileges developing countries to lower cuts is checked, there will be little reduction in the applied rates in many developing countries.

Winners and Losers

Such tariffs, export subsidies, and domestic subsidies have two features in common: they raise prices received by producers in the countries providing them and lower prices in the world market. For example, a tariff or export subsidy set by the EU diverts sales from the EU to the world market, thereby raising the internal EU price and lowering the world price. An EU output subsidy increases the output of the product in the EU and lowers the unit price in the EU and in the rest of the world by less than the subsidy per unit, causing the EU producers' prices and revenue to rise.

Producers in the country employing these interventions necessarily benefit because both the unit price they receive and the total quantity they sell rise in all cases. Not surprisingly, they oppose dismantling these instruments. Countries that import the products subject to these interventions also benefit from reduced world prices. Poor countries that enjoy duty-free access to the markets of tariff-levying countries also benefit because they are able to sell their exports at these countries' internal prices. Thus, they have the same protection as the producers of the tariff-levying countries and are winners, not losers, in the current agricultural regime. This is particularly the case with LDCs, which enjoy duty-free access to the EU market under its Everything But Arms initiative. On the other hand, food-exporting countries such as the members of the Cairns Group, which includes the world's most competitive agricultural producers, are hurt by lower world prices and therefore have the greatest incentive to seek liberalization. For the same reason, the overall impact of the interventions, especially of subsidies, is also negative on the EU. In technical jargon, the terms of trade deteriorate for the EU.

These observations yield some key conclusions. The common assertion that agricultural liberalization in rich countries would bring large benefits to LDCs is mistaken. These states— many of them poor African countries—benefit from the current regime because they can sell their exports at the high EU prices and buy imports at the low world prices. (Cotton is perhaps the sole exception: U.S. subsidies hurt poor countries because the EU tariff on cotton is zero and therefore its internal price for cotton is the same as the world price.) Gains to those developing countries not in the Cairns Group would accrue principally from their own liberalization. The principle of comparative advantage applies just as much to agriculture as to industry. Moreover, because developing countries do not currently enjoy trade preferences in one another's markets, they stand to gain from access there.

Meanwhile, liberalization in developed countries would principally benefit them. Ending their agricultural subsidies would eliminate not only inefficiencies but also the losses from the spillover of the subsidies to the importing countries. Cutting tariffs will generate benefits for their consumers by lowering prices. And countries with a comparative advantage in agriculture—mainly developed countries such as the United States, Canada, Australia, and New Zealand as well as the richer developing countries in the Cairns Group such as Brazil, Argentina, Malaysia, and Indonesia—would benefit from the higher world prices that would follow liberalization in the developed countries.

Gains from the removal of subsidies under the Doha Round, moreover, are likely to be much smaller than previously thought. For one thing, negotiable subsidies have never been as large as has been publicized, and they have declined in importance over the years. Today, export subsidies are in the $3 billion to $5 billion range and domestic subsidies subject to negotiations are well below $100 billion. These numbers are not insignificant, but they are much smaller than commonly believed, making tariffs the more serious barrier to agricultural trade.

Numerous estimates by economists support these conclusions. Careful research shows that the gains to developing countries outside of the Cairns Group from developed-country liberalization would be meager, and that countries that today enjoy preferences in the rich-country markets typically would lose from such reform. Developing countries, especially small ones and those with high initial protection of their own, would benefit more from their own liberalization.

| "The food economy is based on processed
| foods and additives derived from corn."

Agricultural Subsidies Encourage the Overproduction of Unhealthy Food

Amy Frykholm

In the following viewpoint, Amy Frykholm argues that the current farm subsidy program in the United States is contributing to poor nutrition and health problems such as obesity. Frykholm claims that the food the subsidies support is not healthy, nutritious food. Additionally, she claims that the subsidy program supports large agribusiness that focuses on these few unhealthy crops, while destroying small farms both in the United States and abroad. Amy Frykholm is special correspondent for The Christian Century, *a Christian magazine.*

As you read, consider the following questions:

1. According to Frykholm, the bulk of farm subsidies in the United States go to producers of what five crops?

2. What percentage of persistently poor counties in the United States are rural, according to the author?

3. What kinds of changes did the defeated Lugar-Lautenberg reform proposal put forward, according to Frykholm?

A breakfast frequently served at my son's school—where over half the children receive government-supported meals—consists of commercially produced French toast sticks and syrup. The list of ingredients on the package for this meal is as long as this paragraph. It includes not only partially hydrogenated soybean oil and high fructose corn syrup, but also more mystifying additives like gelatinized wheat starch, calcium caseinate, lecithin, guar gum and cellulose gum. The story of how these items arrive at a school cafeteria and are designated as food is a long and complicated one involving the interaction of farmers, government policy makers and the food industry.

Roosevelt's Program

The modern story of why we eat what we eat begins in the 1930s, when President Franklin Roosevelt faced the challenges of the Depression. He saw that many farmers were poor and that one in every five people in the country was undernourished. Farmers and other Americans were too vulnerable, he believed, to the cycles of boom and bust. When crop production was high, prices were too low to support farmers. When crop production was low, farmers didn't have enough to feed themselves, let alone the rest of the nation.

Farmers' vulnerability was the impetus for Roosevelt's reform. "An unprecedented condition calls for new means to rescue agriculture." Roosevelt said as dust storms devastated fields in Oklahoma. The program included a subsidy system to ensure farmers' income and to "reduce the gap between huge surpluses and disastrous shortages." This system was designed to create greater reserves of food that could "help iron out extreme ups and downs of price." Originally more than 100 distinct crops qualified for support.

When Roosevelt signed the Agriculture Adjustment Act and Farm Relief in 1933, he believed he was saving the family farm. At the time, 21 percent of Americans earned their living from farming and one in four Americans lived on a farm. Today that number is less than 2 percent.

Subsidies Today

In the decades that followed, the industrialization of farming changed the subsidy system dramatically. In the 1970s, under Secretary of Agriculture Earl Butz, farm policy sharpened its focus on creating cheap raw materials. It turned farmers from tenders of the land into managers of agribusinesses. Due largely to Butz's reforms, today the bulk of farm subsidies go to producers of only five crops: wheat, soybeans, corn, cotton and rice, and the food economy is based on processed foods and additives derived from corn.

The subsidy program is not so much a means of stabilizing family farms as a way of supporting agribusinesses. Seventy percent of the $21 billion in subsidy payments goes to 10 percent of farmers. In 2005, Riceland Foods Inc. received almost $16 million. Some family farms receive as much as $700,000. Eighty percent of eligible farmers receive an average of $704. In other words, a lot of the money goes to subsidize a very small number of farmers.

American farmers are, as Michael Pollan, author of *The Omnivore's Dilemma*, puts it, "the most productive humans who have ever lived." A small number of farmers grow the food that feeds a nation and many other people around the world. Yet we do not eat much of the food they grow in the form in which they grow it. More than two-thirds of farm products go into livestock feed, and much of the rest must be transformed through manufacturing into the products we consume.

The rise of processed food is linked to what the [former] surgeon general [Richard Carmona] has called an "obesity epidemic" and the rise of lifestyle-related diseases such as heart disease and diabetes. Processed foods offer cheap calories and little nutrition. Our bodies have long been good at digesting apples but hardly know what to do with guar gum or partially hydrogenated vegetable oil. The problem has perhaps most directly affected the poor: calorie-rich food is inexpensive, while the price of fresh foods is increasing. As Kimberly Burge of Bread for the World aptly puts it. "Calories are cheap in the United States—it's nutrients that are expensive."

The Harms of Subsidies

We can see, then, how and why a rather unhealthy breakfast is prepared at my son's school. The production of the wheat and corn in his breakfast are subsidized by the government. The elements are processed and then sold back to the government as part of a nationwide nutrition program.

Schools that attempt to bring high-nutrient food to children can find themselves scolded by the Department of Agriculture for failing to deliver enough calories. Activist and writer Bill McKibben is one of many who sees something wrong here. "Having 'nutrition' programs ride on the back of an unsound agricultural policy—basically tossing the scraps of a crappy food system to the poor—is in nobody's interest in the long run," he says.

Besides encouraging the use of processed food, the subsidy program has had surprisingly negative effects on rural areas. Supporters of subsidies—especially members of Congress— argue that subsidies bring much-needed funds into economically struggling areas. But subsidies do little to stop the trends affecting those areas. As large farms become larger and small farms disappear, the population dwindles. Corporate farmers have little incentive to shop locally, so local economics begin to disappear too. Tamela Walhof, a regional organizer for Bread for the World, says many rural residents have to drive an hour and 15 minutes to the grocery store and bus their children two and half hours to school. Poverty in rural areas outpaces that of urban areas. And poverty in rural areas is more intractable—90 percent of persistently poor counties (counties with high poverty levels for 30 years or more) are rural.

The subsidy program is not only problematic for Americans. It also disrupts the global food economy. By selling corn below cost in the 1990s, the U.S. destroyed about a third of Mexican agriculture, putting a million Mexican farmers out of business. Not incidentally, Mexican immigration to the United States increased 123 percent over the same period. A change in the U.S. pricing and subsidy system might not make enormous differences for small farmers worldwide, but with many of the world's farmers living on less than $1 per day, small differences turn out to be significant. The World Trade Organization has repeatedly reprimanded the U.S. for its practice of subsidizing cotton growers, and it has given Brazil and other countries the right to retaliate.

Finally, the current system does not put a priority on environmental protection or on sustainable agriculture. Industrialized farming means that land is worked harder than it should be. Soils are depleted and the water supply undermined. Perhaps most disturbing, the agricultural system rests, as Pollan observes, "on a sinking sea of petroleum." Food is transported an average of 1,500 miles from the place where it is grown to where it is eaten. Farmers rely on petroleum for pesticides, fertilizers and manufacturing.

Failed Reform Attempts

Many of these issues were discussed when Congress debated the farm bill last year [2007]. It was evident then that an increasing number of people see the subsidy program as an untamed monster. Major reports on the topic appeared in *Time*, the *Washington Post* and the *New York Times*. Yet legislators have little incentive to enact major reforms. What senators in their right minds would oppose subsidy payments that bring money to their regions and their constituents?

One of the reform proposals most hotly debated in the Senate, but ultimately defeated, was the Lugar-Lautenberg Amendment, which would have shifted subsidies to fruit and vegetable growers and cut overall spending on subsidies in order to shift money to conservation, biofuel and nutrition programs. The amendment would have replaced a number of subsidies with an insurance program for farmers. Several other amendments—also defeated—would have capped payments to individual farms (the proposed caps ranged from $250,000 to $750,000). In the end, debate yielded very little in the way of reform.

The exact nature of the reauthorized farm bill has yet to be decided. Disagreements in the Senate and the House as well as disagreements between Congress and the White House make the most likely scenario an extension of the 2002 farm bill for at least a year. This could very well mean that even the small number of reforms and slightly increased funding levels for nutrition fought for in the 2007 legislation will not be enacted. [The 2008 Farm Bill continues many of the commodity programs of 2002.]

In earlier years, when mainline churches and parachurch organizations like Bread for the World lobbied on the farm bill, they emphasized the importance of nutrition programs. During debate on the 2007 farm bill, however, they took a broader approach. They urged a change in the community payment system, arguing that subsidies should go to smaller farms and smaller farmers. They also wanted an end to the trade-distorting subsidies that have devastating consequences on people worldwide. And they wanted to see a redistribution of funds to address conservation, nutrition and global hunger. Leslie Woods of the Washington office of the Presbyterian Church (U.S.A.) says that church groups are now grappling with the lack of success in their reform effort.

Thinking Locally and Globally

Daniel Imhoff, author of *Food Fight: A Citizen's Guide to a Food and Farm Bill,* thinks the debate on farm policy would be more productive if nutrition programs were taken out of the farm bill. The equity and benefits of the subsidy system would be clearer if legislators did not negotiate nutrition programs at the same time that they discussed farm policy. As it is, legislative bodies are "held hostage," he says, with some legislators arguing, "If you don't support my region's subsidies, we won't support your region's nutrition programs." Woods agrees, arguing that the food stamp program helps everyone—it is not an issue that should divide rural areas from urban areas.

Woods, Imhoff and McKibben all argue for a dramatic change in the way that subsidies are allocated. Subsidies should be redirected, McKibben says, toward small farmers and new farmers. "At this point we grow far more corn and soybeans than we need, and far less good food than we should; we have far too few people on the farm; and it's all the result of government policy favoring industrialized agriculture."

McKibben proposes that church groups, which have long been interested in food and hunger issues, start to take malnutrition seriously and link up with farmers' markets and local-food movements in order to begin to create a more equitable system for the distribution of healthy food. Church and parachurch organizations are uniquely poised to make the local, national and global connections that need to be made to create real reform. They have congregants who are educated about world hunger and who are active in local communities.

Some of the most useful proposals come in the form of pilot programs that can be groomed to fit local circumstances, local farmers and local consumers. Such experiments include support for organic farming, for a greater diversity of crops, for changing distribution systems and for supplying nutritious food to institutions. Churches and nonprofit organizations can also be important in this effort because they can offer small grants and loans to support not only direct food services (food pantries and soup kitchens, traditionally), but also the development of sustainable agriculture.

If there were any successes in the debate over the 2007 farm bill, they came in the development of what Imhoff calls literacy. People all over the country started to debate farm policy. "We succeeded in changing the debate," Woods says. "Folks in congregations are more knowledgeable than they were about the effect of farm policy on both local and global markets. Even though we were not able to find a satisfying answer to the problems posed by farm legislation, the conversation is continuing."

To face the challenges of contemporary farming, Americans have to think both locally and globally. We have to connect the food put on our tables and in our lunch sacks to the fields we drive by on our vacations and to fields and feedlots we will never see. The challenge of creating an equitable farm policy that serves farmers and consumers is just as great as it was in the 1930s. The consequences of not facing up to the challenge may be even more dire.

> "These subsidies undercut developing-
> world producers and distort the market
> for both U.S. consumers and their
> counterparts overseas."

Agricultural Subsidies Worsen the Global Food Shortage Crisis

Washington Times

In the following viewpoint, the Washington Times *claims that worldwide high food prices are the result of economic and structural factors such as U.S. agricultural policy, which gives out subsidies to U.S. farmers of a few crops. The author points to the alarming consequences of increasing food prices in 2008, including food riots, rampant inflation of food prices, and the threat of a hunger epidemic. The* Washington Times *is a daily newspaper in Washington, DC.*

As you read, consider the following questions:

1. According to the author, how much did the cost of rice rise in Sierra Leone during the food crisis discussed?

2. How much food aid did the United States supply in 2007?

3. One-third of the U.S. farm bill goes toward what market-distorting program, according to the author?

In the United States, spiraling food and energy prices mean shock at the gas pump and a per-customer cap on Sam's Club rice purchases. But food-price hikes in Haiti, Egypt, Cameroon, Burkina Faso, Yemen and Mexico, to name a few nations, mean hunger, rioting or even death.

In February [2008], months before significant Western attention to the food crisis, 40 people died in food riots in the West African nation of Cameroon. In Burkina Faso, the third stop on U.N. Secretary-General Ban Ki-moon's tour of West Africa this week [April 21–24, 2008], a central market in the capital was torched in March by rioters angry with the rising cost of living. The cost of rice has risen 300 percent in Sierra Leone, another site of the recent months' riots. Three weeks ago in politically repressed Egypt, riots broke out at the center of the country's textile industry north of Cairo. Late last week, in Thailand, the world's leading rice exporter, prices rose five percent to a level triple last year's, prompting fears of deeper rice shortages and hoarding.

The first of Haiti's recent food riots were reported three weeks ago. The poorest country in the Western Hemisphere and a periodic source of refugees to the United States and surrounding countries, Haiti has suffered more than 50 percent increases in rice, beans and fruit prices in the last year. Rioters struck when demonstrations in the southern town of Les Cayes turned into violent melees. At least four were killed and 20 were wounded. Other incidents followed. Shots have been exchanged with United Nations peacekeepers. The 4-year-old Brazilian-led U.N. Stabilization Mission in Haiti, which consists of nearly 9,000 multinational police and military personnel and another 1,800 civilians, has already grown repeatedly to meet the challenges of pre-food crisis security conditions now worsened by a deteriorating economic environment.

Resolving the Crisis

Faced with today's high food prices, each government has tended to look at the issues from its own narrow perspective. That's understandable, but when governments have gotten together in efforts to deal with these problems in concert they haven't done well either.... Agriculture has been pivotal to those talks because governments have already made such progress on reducing trade barriers on other goods and services, and because the Doha Round [of trade talks], was aimed at helping the world's poorest, which requires helping their farmers become more profitable. Subsidies by rich countries are a chief obstacle to success.

David G. Victor, Newsweek, *July 7–14, 2008.*

Josette Sheeran, executive director of the United Nations World Food Program [WFP], warns of a "silent tsunami that respects no borders." Rising prices, she said, threaten to "plunge more than 100 million people on every continent into hunger"—people who were not in danger six months ago.

The understandable urge in the West is to "do something," most immediately in the form of food shipments, which will feed some of the hungry in the short term if managed properly. A day after World Bank president and [George W.] Bush administration veteran Robert Zoellick called on the developed world to "put our money where our mouth is," the Department of Agriculture released $200 million in emergency food aid from a food reserve it manages known as the Bill Emerson Humanitarian Trust. The United States, already the world's largest provider of food aid, supplied $2.1 billion worth in 2007. Mrs. Sheeran's WFP has called for an additional $500 million in food assistance by May 1. The [Bill & Melinda] Gates Foundation also boosted its own food aid by 50 percent to $240 million this year. There are others.

But the real fixes are economic and structural. Food aid is a temporary solution. The current [passed May 22, 2008] farm bill stalled in Congress is one excellent place to begin. About two-thirds of this bill funds food stamps and other nutritional programs which should be separated out from the offensive, market-distorting components of the legislation. Most of the remaining one-third will exacerbate the world food crisis with unnecessary subsidies and largesse for U.S. cotton, rice, soybean, corn, and wheat producers. These subsidies undercut developing-world producers and distort the market for both U.S. consumers and their counterparts overseas. The only beneficiaries are the producers themselves, who, far from the image of the American farmer of yore, often run multimillion-dollar agribusinesses. Unneeded farm aid is a bipartisan problem and a bipartisan embarrassment.

Ethanol is another key aggravating factor. The fivefold increase in the use of biofuels mandated by Congress must be jettisoned. Currently, about a fifth of the U.S. corn crop is converted into fuel. Congress failed to realize when it acted that the conversion of corn into fuel matters hugely on the margin in global markets for foodstuffs. Thankfully, a global backlash against ethanol is developing in Europe. It would be welcome news if it soon reaches the United States.

Periodical Bibliography

The following articles have been selected to supplement the diverse views presented in this chapter.

Max Borders and H. Sterling Burnett
"Farm Subsidies: Devastating the World's Poor and the Environment," National Center for Policy Analysis (NCPA), March 24, 2006. www.ncpa.org.

Christopher D. Cook
"Farm Bill: Making America Fat and Polluted, One Subsidy at a Time," *Christian Science Monitor*, April 23, 2008.

Economist
"A Harvest of Disgrace," May 22, 2008.

Robert McMahon and Lee Hudson Teslik
"The Doha Trade Talks," Council on Foreign Relations, February 22, 2008, www.cfr.org.

Anuradha Mittal
"Harvest of Suicides: How Global Trade Rules Are Driving Indian Farmers to Despair," *Earth Island Journal*, Spring 2008.

Dan Morgan and Gilbert M. Gaul
"Big Profits from Crop Insurance Criticized," *Washington Post*, May 4, 2007.

Deroy Murdock
"U.S. Farm Subsidies Smack Mother Nature," *Cincinnati Post*, September 28, 2007.

Bob Peace
"The Food on Our Tables: The Flaws of U.S. Agricultural Policy," *America*, January 19, 2009.

Brian M. Riedl
"How Farm Subsidies Harm Taxpayers, Consumers, and Farmers, Too," *Backgrounder*, No. 2043, Heritage Foundation, June 19, 2007. www.heritage.org.

Heather Schoonover and Mark Muller
"Food Without Thought: How U.S. Farm Policy Contributes to Obesity," Institute for Agriculture and Trade Policy, March 2006. www.iatp.org.

George Wehrfritz and Stefan Thei
"It's the Stupid Politics," *Newsweek International*, May 19, 2008.

CHAPTER 3

Should Agricultural Subsidies Be Eliminated?

Chapter Preface

Since its inception in 1995, the World Trade Organization (WTO) has been the organization for international trade negotiations. The goal of the organization is to remove trade barriers and oversee international trade. As of July 2008, the WTO had 153 members representing over 95% of world trade. In 2001, trade ministers launched the Doha round of trade negotiations, called the Doha Development Round, initially with a deadline for final agreements by January 1, 2005. The objective of the Doha Round is to lower trade barriers around the world, but as of 2009, talks have stalled over disagreements on major issues. Issues related to agricultural trade dominate the disagreements, with regulations on agricultural subsidies being one of the main stumbling blocks to agreement among nations.

The Doha Ministerial Declaration of November 20, 2001, set out the directive for the negotiations, noting that the negotiations should be aimed at "substantial improvements in market access; reductions of, with a view to phasing out, all forms of export subsidies; and substantial reductions in trade-distorting domestic support." The central focus, then, is to have all nations allow fair access to their products by reducing or eliminating economic support that governments grant through financial aid given to farmers domestically and through payments directed at encouraging export of the nation's products. Additionally, the declaration makes special note that different treatment might be warranted for developed versus developing countries:

> Special and differential treatment for developing countries
> shall be an integral part of all elements of the negotiations
> and shall be embodied in the schedules of concessions and
> commitments and as appropriate in the rules and disciplines
> to be negotiated, so as to be operationally effective and to

enable developing countries to effectively take account of their development needs, including food security and rural development.

Despite the directive, after over seven years of negotiations, an agreement has not been reached regarding agricultural subsidies.

Although the WTO takes the position that agricultural subsidies should be largely reduced or eliminated, the issue is far from settled. In this chapter, policy experts, columnists, specialists, and academics debate this contentious issue that continues to plague the Doha Development Round discussions.

| "The time is ripe for unilaterally remov-
ing those distorting trade policies."

U.S. Agricultural Subsidies Should Be Eliminated

Daniel Griswold, Stephen Slivinski, and Christopher Preble

In the following viewpoint, Daniel Griswold, Stephen Slivinski, and Christopher Preble give several reasons why farm subsidies and other trade barriers ought to be eradicated. The authors cite such varied harms—which they claim result from agricultural policy that includes a farm subsidy program—as higher costs of goods for consumers and businesses, environmental damage, lack of agricultural diversity, and harm to poor countries. Daniel Griswold is director of the Center for Trade Policy Studies, Stephen Slivinski is director of budget studies, and Christopher Preble is director of foreign policy studies, all at the Cato Institute.

As you read, consider the following questions:

1. How may sugar refineries have closed in the United States in the last two decades, according to the authors, and what is the cause they cite?

Daniel Griswold, Stephen Slivinski, and Christopher Preble, "6 Reasons to Kill Farm Subsidies and Trade Barriers: A No-Nonsense Reform Strategy," *Reason*, vol. 37, February 2006, pp. 42–49. Copyright © 2006 by Reason Foundation, 3415 S. Sepulveda Blvd., Suite 400, Los Angeles, CA 90034, www.reason.com. Reproduced by permission.

2. The authors use what example to support their view that agricultural water subsidies prop up enterprises that waste scarce water resources?

3. According to the authors, does the United States spend more money on subsidies and tariffs, or foreign aid to the developing world?

A merica's agricultural policies have remained fundamentally unchanged for nearly three-quarters of a century. The U.S. government continues to subsidize the production of rice, milk, sugar, cotton, peanuts, tobacco, and other commodities, while restricting imports to maintain artificially high domestic prices. The competition and innovation that have changed the face of the planet have been effectively locked out of America's farm economy by politicians who fear farm voters more than the dispersed consumers who subsidized them.

The time is ripe for unilaterally removing those distorting trade policies. . . .

Food Prices for American Families

The foremost reason to curtail farm protectionism is to benefit American consumers. By shielding the domestic market from global competition, government farm programs raise the cost of food and with it the overall cost of living. According to the Organization for Economic Cooperation and Development, the higher domestic food prices caused by U.S. farm programs transferred $16.2 billion from American consumers to domestic agricultural producers in 2004. That amounts to an annual "food tax" per household of $146. This consumer tax is paid over and above what we dole out to farmers through the federal budget.

American consumers pay more than double the world price for sugar. The federal sugar program guarantees domestic producers a take of 22.9 cents per pound for beet sugar and 18 cents for cane sugar, while the world spot price for raw cane sugar is currently about 10 cents per pound. A 2000 study by the General Accounting Office estimated that Americans paid an extra $1.9 billion a year for sugar due to import quotas alone.

American families also pay more for their milk, butter, and cheese, thanks to federal dairy price supports and trade barriers. The federal government administers a byzantine system of domestic price supports, marketing orders, import controls, export subsidies, and domestic and international giveaway programs. According to the U.S. International Trade Commission, between 2000 and 2002 the average domestic price of nonfat dry milk was 23 percent higher than the world price, cheese 37 percent higher, and butter more than double. Trade policies also drive up prices for peanuts, cotton, beef, orange juice, canned tuna, and other products.

These costs are compounded by escalating tariffs based on the amount of processing embodied in a product. If the government allowed lower market prices for commodity inputs, processed foods would be substantially cheaper. Lifting sugar protection, for example, would apply downward pressure on the prices we pay for candy, soft drinks, bakery goods, and other sugar-containing products.

The burden of higher domestic food costs falls disproportionately on poor households. Farm protections act as a regressive tax, with higher prices at the grocery store negating some or all of the income support the government seeks to deliver via programs such as food stamps.

If American farm subsidies and trade barriers were significantly reduced, millions of American households would enjoy higher real incomes.

Cost and Exports for American Companies

Producers who export goods to the rest of the world and manufacturers who use agricultural inputs would also stand to benefit significantly from farm reform. So would their employees.

When government intervention raises domestic prices for raw materials and other commodities, it imposes higher costs on "downstream" users in the supply chain. Those higher costs can mean higher prices for consumers, reduced global competitiveness for American exporters, lower sales, less investment, and ultimately fewer employment opportunities and lower pay in the affected industries. Artificially high commodity prices drive domestic producers abroad to seek cheaper inputs—or out of business altogether.

In the last two decades, the number of sugar refineries in the U.S. has dwindled from 23 to eight, largely because of the doubled price of domestic raw sugar. During the last decade thousands of jobs have been lost in the confectionary industry, with losses especially heavy in the Chicago area. Expensive food also hurts restaurants.

Lowering Trade Barriers

Enterprises outside the food business would benefit from farm reform as well. Rich countries' agricultural trade barriers remain the single greatest obstacle to a comprehensive World Trade Organization (WTO) agreement on trade liberalization. The current round of talks, the Doha Development Round, came to a halt in Cancun in 2003 when the Group of 20 developing countries demanded more serious farm reform by the rich countries as an essential precondition. Any progress at the December 2005 meeting in Hong Kong and beyond will depend on real progress in cutting U.S. farm subsidies and trade barriers.

A successful Doha Round would lower trade barriers for a whole swath of industrial products and services. A 2001 study by Drusilla Brown at Tuffs University and Alan Deardorff and Robert Stern at the University of Michigan estimated that even a one-third cut in tariffs on agriculture, industry, and services would boost annual global production by $613 billion, including $177 billion in the United States—or about

$1,700 per American household. Some of the country's most competitive sectors, including information technology, financial services, insurance, and consulting, probably would increase their share of global markets if the Doha Round were successful. Farm reform remains the key.

A common argument against liberalization is that the U.S. should hold onto its agricultural tariffs as "bargaining chips" in WTO negotiations. The worry is that if we were to dismantle our barriers unilaterally, other countries would lose any incentive to give up theirs.

But reducing protectionism would not primarily be a "concession" to other countries. It would be a favor to ourselves. In the process we would set a good example and create good will in global negotiations, inviting other countries to join us in realizing the benefits of lower domestic food costs.

Cost for U.S. Taxpayers

Agricultural reform also would reduce the cost of government. The Office of Management and Budget estimates that taxpayers shelled out an expected $26 billion in direct agricultural subsidies in fiscal year 2005—the biggest single-year subsidy bill since 1986. Just nine years ago [in 1997], Congress promised to phase out farm subsidies by 2003. Instead they've reached near-record highs.

Subsidy levels before 1996 were set by a formula that triggered an increase when crop prices fell. Starting in 1995, crop prices began to rise, resulting in lower payments from the federal government. The Freedom to Farm Act, passed in 1996 when commodity prices were high and demand for subsidies low, ended the price support program and replaced it with a declining fixed payment unrelated to market prices. Payouts were scheduled to drop from $5.6 billion in 1996 to $4 billion by 2002 and then disappear.

But Congress reversed course in 1998, when crop prices began to decline, passing an "emergency" supplemental bill that raised total farm subsidies to $12.4 billion. Subsequent supplementals hiked handouts to new heights, totaling more than $76 billion between 1999 and 2002, a whopping $57 billion more than the Freedom to Farm Act originally mandated.

In May 2002, President George W. Bush hammered the final nail into Freedom to Farm, signing a six-year appropriation that revived the old price support program. Taxpayers have coughed up $55.5 billion in the three fiscal years since. For the same money Congress paid to farmers during the "phase-out" period between 1995 and 2003, the federal government could have purchased outright more than a quarter of the country's farms.

Subsidizing Agribusiness

Yet two-thirds of American farmers don't even receive subsidies. So where does all that tax money go? Mainly to large agribusinesses and the richest family farmers. In 2003, the most recent year for which comprehensive statistics are available, the top 10 percent of all subsidy recipients gobbled up 68 percent of the money, and the top 5 percent got 55 percent.

Take, for instance, Riceland Foods in Stuttgart, Arkansas, the largest single recipient of farm welfare. In 2003 it received $68.9 million in subsidies for producing rice, soybeans, wheat, and corn—more than all the farmers in Rhode Island, Hawaii, Alaska, New Hampshire, Connecticut, Massachusetts, Maine, Nevada, and New Jersey combined.

The second-largest recipient of farm welfare in 2003 was Producers Rice Mill, also in Stuttgart, Arkansas, which received $51.4 million. The agricultural welfare rolls also include many *Fortune* 500 companies, such as Archer Daniels Midland and International Paper, plus corporations most people don't associate with farming, such as Chevron, Caterpillar, and Electronic Data Systems.

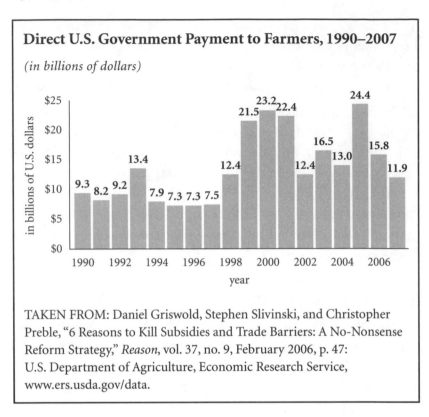

Direct U.S. Government Payment to Farmers, 1990–2007

(in billions of dollars)

TAKEN FROM: Daniel Griswold, Stephen Slivinski, and Christopher
Preble, "6 Reasons to Kill Subsidies and Trade Barriers: A No-Nonsense
Reform Strategy," *Reason*, vol. 37, no. 9, February 2006, p. 47:
U.S. Department of Agriculture, Economic Research Service,
www.ers.usda.gov/data.

From the taxpayer's perspective, there is no good reason
why the federal government should continue to subsidize
farmers or companies, especially those that can remain profitable on their own.

Environmental Damage

The distortions and perverse incentives of U.S. agricultural
policies have encouraged practices that damage the environment. Trade barriers and subsidies stimulate production on
marginal land, leading to overuse of pesticides, fertilizers, and
other effluents. A central if unstated purpose of American
farm policy is to promote production of commodities that
would not be economical under competitive, free market conditions. This often means emphasizing crops better grown
elsewhere, requiring more chemical assistance.

Overuse of fertilizers and pesticides adds to runoff that pollutes rivers, lakes, and oceans. According to the World Resources Institute, agriculture is the biggest source of river and lake pollutants in the United States. A study by the Environmental Protection Agency found that 72 percent of U.S. rivers and 56 percent of lakes it surveyed suffer from agriculture-related pollution. Areas of the Gulf of Mexico have become "dead zones" because of the runoff from farms in the Midwest. Even where fertilizers and pesticides are not used intensively, the mere act of plowing soil eliminates forest and grass cover, leaving soil exposed for weeks at a time and vulnerable to erosion. Erosion can build up silt in nearby rivers and downstream lakes.

Domestic sugar protection has maintained a concentration of producers in central Florida who have used up water from the endangered Florida Everglades while spitting back phosphorous content far above the level consistent with maintaining the surrounding ecosystem. The high runoff has seriously reduced periphyton, such as algae, that supports birds and other animal life. Congress has spent billions to repair the damage caused to the Everglades by the protected sugar industry.

Farm programs also waste scarce water resources, especially in the arid West. Agricultural water subsidies alone amount to around $2 billion annually, propping up such uneconomical enterprises as growing cotton in the Arizona desert.

Finally, farm programs crowd out more environmentally friendly land uses by artificially driving up land prices. A sizeable share of the increased income that protection and subsidies deliver to farms becomes "capitalized" through higher land values, because the subsidies increase the stream of income that land can produce. Higher prices for farmland, in turn, render it more expensive to acquire and maintain environmental preserves, parkland, forests, or other land use alternatives that would be more likely to preserve habitats and biodiversity. By keeping marginal farmland under cultivation, the government has slowed the trend of reforestation.

When New Zealand dramatically reduced farm trade barriers and subsidies in the mid-1980s, farmland values fell sharply, allowing marginal land to return to such uses as forestry and eco-tourism. The use of fertilizers declined, along with overgrazing and soil erosion.

Protection Limits Diversity

Federal farm programs actually work against the interests of many farmers. Growers, especially the two-thirds who don't receive subsidies, pay a heavy price through lost export opportunities from high trade barriers abroad. Agriculture exporters face average foreign tariffs that are several times higher than the average tariffs on manufactured products. The most promising opportunity to lower those barriers is the Doha Round, which won't achieve a breakthrough until the rich countries stop trying to prop up their farms.

If global barriers to farm trade were removed, the World Bank estimates, worldwide farm exports would be 74 percent higher in 2015 than they would otherwise. American farmers would be among the biggest winners: Comprehensive reform would mean an additional $88 billion in annual U.S. farm exports by 2015 and an additional $28 billion in farm imports, for a net $60 billion surplus.

Protection has not served the long-term interests of even the most protected farm sectors. Barriers to commodity imports discourage diversification of production into higher-value-added items and retard development of the food processing industry. They discourage domestic consumption and encourage the use of lower-priced substitutes, undermining the protected sectors' own domestic market share.

Artificially high prices for sugar, for example, have contributed to a long-term decline in domestic sugar consumption. Today Americans consume about 40 percent less sugar per capita than they did when consumption was at its peak in 1972. Domestic sugar has been replaced on the menu not by imports but by U.S.-made substitutes such as high-fructose corn syrup and low-calorie sweeteners such as Splenda. Sugar's share of the domestic sweetener market has been cut in half since 1967.

Experience shows that American farmers can thrive in free and open markets. American farmers profitably produce lettuce, celery, cauliflower, potatoes, almonds, pistachios, apples, pears, cherries, melons, blueberries, grapes, and hundreds of other specialty crops without guaranteed prices or protected markets. The impact of farm subsidies on land prices makes growing these unprotected crops more expensive, and barriers caused by the protection of other crops block exports.

The experience of New Zealand and Australia demonstrates that farmers can survive and thrive without significant state support. Both of those countries enacted sweeping, unilateral reforms, including the elimination of import barriers and domestic price support subsidies. As expected, some farms have gone out of business, but many others have changed their operations to meet consumer demand. The result has been not a massive downsizing of the agriculture sector but a surge of innovation, productivity, and output.

Damage to Poor Countries

The collective effect of American farm policies is to depress the income of agricultural producers worldwide, exacerbating poverty in areas such as sub-Saharan Africa and Central Asia, where people are heavily dependent on agriculture.

The frustration and despair caused by these policies undermine American security. Many people who depend on agriculture for their survival, both as a source of nourishment and a means of acquiring wealth, perceive U.S. farm policy as part of an anti-American narrative in which Washington wants to keep the rest of the world locked in poverty. Indeed, in a survey of anti-American sentiment around the world, the Pew Research Center found a majority of respondents in more than a dozen countries were convinced that U.S. farm and trade policies increased the "poverty gap" worldwide. These sentiments transcended geographic, ethnic, or religious boundaries. In such an environment, terrorist ringleaders find fertile ground for their message of hate and violence.

Nicholas Stern, chief economist at the World Bank, is blunt about America's leadership role. "It is hypocritical to preach the advantages of free trade and free markets," Stern told the U.N. publication *Africa Recovery*, "and then erect obstacles in precisely those markets in which developing countries have a comparative advantage." Johan Norberg, of the Swedish think tank Timbro, argues that farm protection in developed countries amounts to a "deliberate and systematic means of undermining the very type of industry in which the developing countries do have comparative advantages."

American subsidies and tariffs amount to much more money than its foreign aid to the developing world. According to Oxfam, "in crop year 2002, the U.S. government provided $3.4 billion in total subsidies to the cotton sector," including about 25,000 growers. "To put this figure into perspective," Oxfam says, "it is nearly twice the total amount of U.S. foreign aid given to sub-Saharan Africa. It is also more than the GDP [Gross Domestic Product] of Benin, Burkina Faso, or Chad, the main cotton-producing countries in the region." The subsidies drive down world cotton prices, costing developing countries billions of dollars in lost export earnings.

Poor countries don't want our pity; they want our respect. To the extent that American security depends on the expansion of liberal democratic institutions and free market economics, Washington must be particularly sensitive to policies that exacerbate poverty in the developing world.

A Call for Reform

For the sake of our broader national interest, Congress and the president should reduce, with the ultimate goal of eliminating, all agricultural trade barriers and production subsidies. The long-term interests of Americans as consumers, producers, taxpayers, and citizens of the world should not be sacrificed for the short-term interests of a small minority of farmers. . . .

A farm bill with deep cuts in subsidies and trade barriers would save U.S. taxpayers and consumers tens of billions of dollars during the next decade while potentially opening markets abroad for tens of billions more in American exports across the economy. Congress and the president should seize the opportunity to bring America's farm sector into the nurturing sunlight of an open global market.

"*Subsidies don't cause overproduction—
and withdrawing subsidies won't end
overproduction.*"

Eliminating U.S. Agricultural Subsidies Is Not a Good Solution

Tom Philpott

*In the following viewpoint, Tom Philpott argues that agricultural
subsidies are wrongly blamed for a host of problems. Philpott
claims that overproduction is the cause of many problems, such
as obesity, as well as the cause of the subsidies themselves. Eliminating subsidies, he concludes, will do nothing to address the
problem with U.S. agricultural policy. Tom Philpott is food editor at* Grist, *an online environmental news and commentary
magazine, and founder of Maverick Farms, a sustainable-
agriculture non-profit farm located in the Blue Ridge Mountains
of western North Carolina.*

As you read, consider the following questions:

1. What does Philpott identify as the fundamental problem
   of U.S. agriculture?

2. According to the author, how do large-scale farmers tend to respond to lower prices?

3. What message increasingly sent from the federal government to farmers between the early 1970s and mid-1990s needs to change, according to Philpott?

A lot of people, myself among them, have spent substantial time this year [2007] trying to demystify the 2007 Farm Bill. But as it lurches into its stretch run—with passage possible by year-end—I fear that the bill [passed in 2008 as the Food, Conservation, and Energy Act of 2008] is more shrouded in mystery than ever, even among sustainable-agriculture advocates.

Here's what we can all agree on: Late last month [October 25, 2007] the Senate Agriculture Committee passed a version of the bill that would generally preserve the crop subsidies that have become so infamous. It would also add funding to some important conservation and nutrition programs, the result of hard lobbying by sustainable-ag and anti-hunger activists. . . .

The proposal has unleashed a hailstorm of criticism in sustainable-agriculture, public-health, and environmental circles, where hope had swelled for policy reform. Anger focused primarily on the version's commodity title, which—like the House version passed last spring—would continue delivering billions of dollars to producers of a few crops, mainly corn, cotton, wheat, rice, and soybeans.

The Focus on Subsidies

Writing in the *New York Times* op-ed page on Sunday [November 4, 2007], Michael Pollan gave eloquent voice to the dismay. The boost in conservation funding was fine and well, Pollan wrote, but "[a]s long as the commodity title remains untouched, the way we eat will remain unchanged."

Here is precisely where the complexities of our farm policy blind even its most well informed critics. The commodity title has been credited with awesome power—it has been said to underwrite everything from the obesity epidemic to the explosion in CAFOs [Concentrated Animal Feeding Operations] in the late 1990s to the dead zone in the Gulf of Mexico. In its spare time, it's steamrolling farmers in Mexico, Africa, and elsewhere.

True, all of those maladies can be traced directly to agricultural overproduction, mainly of corn. *But subsidies don't cause overproduction—and withdrawing subsidies won't end overproduction.* With all due respect to Pollan, gutting the commodity title probably wouldn't change much about the way we eat—or do much to curtail the heavy applications of nitrogen fertilizer in the Corn Belt that are fouling up the Gulf, or end the scourge of CAFOs, or curtail the dumping of agriculture commodities into the global south.

By focusing their ire on subsidies, Pollan and a host of critics—including OxFam, Environmental Defense, the Environmental Working Group, and others—are fixating on a *symptom* of overproduction, not the *cause*. They're rallying around an alternative proposal from Sens. Richard Lugar (R-Ind.) and Frank Lautenberg (D-N.J.) that would abolish subsidies but likely fail to address the fundamental problem of U.S. agriculture: maximum production of a few commodity crops.

The Tendency Toward Overproduction

In their paper criticizing the 2002 Farm Bill, "Rethinking U.S. Agriculture Policy," the agriculture economist [Daryll] Ray and his colleagues provide a lucid explanation of overproduction. It goes like this: Farm productivity tends to grow much faster than the demand for food. In a mature economy like the United States, food demand grows at about the rate of population. But agricultural productivity—juiced up by genetically modified seeds, the latest high-tech equipment, pesticides, artificial fertilizers, etc.—tends to grow more rapidly.

In 1926, for example, an acre of corn yielded around 25 bushels. Today, farmers routinely squeeze upwards of 150 bushels from that acre, a six-fold increase. Other major staple crops like wheat and soy have undergone similar booms in yield per acre. But over the same period, population grew by a factor of less than three. So farms have been churning out food way faster than people can consume it, leading to huge surpluses.

This tendency toward overproduction, when managed well, actually benefits society. As Ray and his collaborators put it, "Given that food is essential to life, it is urgent that the productive capacity of agriculture continue to stay well ahead of needs." But for at least 20 or so years now, overproduction has been used to create dubious but profitable products like corn-based ethanol, high-fructose corn syrup, and meat, dairy, and eggs from confined animals.

According to conventional Farm Bill critics, ending subsidies will fix all that. After farmers are subjected to the rigor of the free market, these critics say, booming yields won't be a problem. When farmers overproduce, this line of thinking has it, the price of the commodity drops, signaling that they should plant less the next year. And anyway, foreign countries—especially in the global south, where populations are rising fast—can be counted on to buy up some of that surplus, especially if the latest WTO [World Trade Organization] trade negotiations, known as the Doha round, succeed in prying open markets.

Ending Subsidies Will Not Solve Overpopulation

There are two problems with that scenario. The first is that farmers—especially large-scale ones with established markets in only one or two crops—tend to respond to lower prices by

Unique Market Characteristics of Agriculture

The agricultural sector and particularly crops is distinct from most other economic sectors in a number of crucial ways. The price elasticity of supply and demand are not sufficient to bring about a timely equilibration of the market. Just as a diabetic does not purchase more insulin in response to a price decline, so most people do not increase their aggregate food intake from three meals a day to four in response to lower prices. A decline in the price of lumber may stimulate more do-it-yourselfers to take on the weekend project of building a new deck, but lower prices do not significantly increase the aggregate demand for food. Lower prices may stimulate people to eat out more often and to pay for additional processing of the foods they prepare at home, but they do not significantly increase total food consumption. . . .

One of the little recognized factors in low crop prices is the role of public investment in research and extension in increasing supply at a faster rate than population growth. The inevitable result of this supply increase in the face of an inelastic demand is lower prices.

Daryll E. Ray and Harwood D. Schaffer,
"Targeting Policy Toward Each of Three Agricultures,"
Agricultural Policy Analysis Center (APAC),
November 2004, www.agpolicy.org.

planting *more*, hoping to make up in volume what they're losing in price. They also scramble to invest in productivity-enhancing technology like the latest John Deere combine or seed variety from Monsanto. And when those decisions are multiplied across hundreds of thousands of farms across the Midwest, you get lower prices leading to more production and more downward pressure on prices.

The second problem with the free-market view involves using exports as a safety valve for our overproduction. While it's certainly true that international trade talks and binational pacts can be used to ram open markets for U.S. agriculture commodities, other countries have the same idea. Brazil's production of both soy and corn has exploded since the early 1990s, bolstered by investment from U.S. and European agribusiness, the USDA [U.S. Department of Agriculture] reports. Argentine corn production is on a similar trajectory.

In short, the effort to "feed the world" with U.S. agriculture surpluses has been seriously hindered by competition from countries where land and labor is cheaper and the growing season is longer. And that's something that the WTO talks, NAFTA, CAFTA, and other agreements can't fix. And as nations like Brazil and Argentina crank out more product, we can expect to get more pressure on U.S. farmers to invest in productivity and jack up yields.

So the end of subsidies won't likely curtail a global push to maximize production of a few commodities by lashing the earth with chemicals, a trend that's only been exacerbated by the biofuel boom. (Cynics will note that the same two commodities whose overproduction underpins our food system—corn and soy—have been deemed the feedstocks of choice for biofuel, even though both leave much to be desired in that regard.)

The lack of a direct connection between subsidies and overproduction probably explains why the agribusiness lobby is not defending the commodity title in the current Farm Bill debate. The voice for preserving subsidies has come from large-scale farmers themselves, mostly through the American Farm Bureau Federation. They figure that since prices look set to drop long-term, they had better not negotiate away what has become an important source of income.

What Agribusiness Wants

Sustainable-food advocates fighting the Farm Bureau on this point have an unexpected ally: the Bush Administration, which has been renouncing subsidies for a couple of years now. Did [George W.] Bush read [Pollan's] *Omnivore's Dilemma* and suddenly become a critic of the industrial-food system? Not likely.

Over the summer I asked Ferd Hoefner, executive director of the Sustainable Agriculture Coalition, what agenda agribusiness giants like Archer Daniels Midland [ADM] and Cargill are pushing for the Farm Bill. Hoefner has been engaged in farm bill fights since the 1970s. "It's basically the Bush plan," he said. Bush's proposal for the farm bill, released last spring, included steep cuts in subsidies. Agribusiness, it seems, would like to see the commodity title dismantled—it's holding up progress on the Doha round of trade talks, which would increase global trade in ag commodities. Countries in the global south are refusing to open their markets to U.S. goods until the subsidies fall, and countries like Archer Daniels Midland are eager to comply.

In fact, Bush and his right-hand man in the USDA, former ADM flack Chuck Conner, have threatened to veto the current version of the farm bill—precisely because of subsidies [though it passed by Congress overriding Bush's veto].

The Wrong Message

After the Great Depression, which involved a collapse in farm prices brought on by a spasm of overproduction, U.S. farm policy sought to help farmers manage supply decisions in an era of booming productivity gains. All of that changed between the early 1970s and the mid-1990s, when the message from the federal government to farmers increasingly became: produce as much as you can.

Real positive reform in federal farm policy will come from changing that message. If the momentum generated by the sustainable-food movement works to slash subsidies without reforming other aspects of policy, money now earmarked for supporting agriculture will go up in smoke in Iraq—likely gone from the USDA budget forever. And the problems of overproduction will persist.

But we'll need the money currently in the commodity title to remain available for supporting farming. It could be used to dramatically expand conservation measures, which give farmers incentives to make more judicious planting decisions; and to reinvest in local and regional food-production infra-structure, which has been dismantled over the past several decades. And that agenda, I hope, will be the focus of organizing for the next farm bill in 2012. Given that the terms of the debate presently seem stuck on subsidy preservers (the Farm Bureau) and subsidy cutters (Bush, Environmental Defense, etc.), that looks like the best-case scenario—though there are measures, like the proposed Dorgan-Grassley amendment [a measure limiting farm subsidy payments that failed to pass], that could improve things at the margins.

I *"Farmers are now wealthier than ever."*

U.S. Farmers Do Not Need Agricultural Subsidies to Survive

Brian M. Riedl

In the following viewpoint, Brian M. Riedl argues that the farm-subsidy system within the current farm bill, The Food, Conservation, and Energy Act of 2008, does not make sense. Riedl contends that farmers today are wealthier than ever and, given this, they do not need the generous farm subsidies that have few caps on income and are handed out regardless of crop price. Brian M. Riedl is senior policy analyst and Grover Hermann Fellow in Federal Budgetary Affairs at the Thomas A. Roe Institute for Economic Policy Studies at the Heritage Foundation.

As you read, consider the following questions:

1. According to Riedl, what is the farm bill income cap for agricultural subsidies in the form of direct payments?

2. From which three sources of the budget must increased farm subsidies come, according to the author?

Brian M. Riedl, "Seven Reasons to Veto the Farm Bill; Backgrounder No. 2134," *Heritage Foundation*, Backgrounder, May 12, 2008, pp. 1–5. Copyright © 2008 The Heritage Foundation. Reproduced by permission.

3. What does the author identify as the true challenge for farmers in the twenty-first century?

The case against the current farm-subsidy system is a strong one. For example:

- Farm subsidies are intended to alleviate farmer poverty, but the majority of subsidies go to commercial farms, which report an average income of $200,000 and a net worth of nearly $2 million.

- Farm subsidies are supposedly needed to keep farmers afloat, yet 90 percent of all subsidies go to growers of just five crops (wheat, cotton, corn, soybeans, and rice). Farms producing the majority of farm products (including fruits, vegetables, beef, and poultry) survive without subsidies.

- Farm subsidies are intended to raise farmer incomes by making up for low crop prices. Instead, subsidies promote overproduction, lowering prices even further. Expensive programs to restrict plantings are then implemented to raise prices again. Ethanol mandates raise prices further.

- Farm subsidies are intended to help struggling family farmers. Instead, they harm those farmers by excluding them from most subsidies; financing the consolidation of small, individually owned farms into business conglomerates; and raising land values to levels that prevent young people from entering farming.

- Farm subsidies allegedly are intended to be consumer- and taxpayer-friendly, but they cost Americans billions of dollars each year in higher taxes and higher food costs.

The farm bill [enacted into law as The Food, Conservation, and Energy Act of 2008] does not address any of these shortcomings. Washington would continue to spend approximately $25 billion annually to subsidize a small, elite group of farmers through policies that do nothing to help the farm economy.

Farm Incomes Shatter Records

The U.S. Department of Agriculture estimates that net farm income will reach a record $92.3 billion in 2008—a 56 percent increase over 2006. The $89,434 average household income for farmers significantly exceeds the national average. Additionally, crop land values soared another 14 percent last year [2007] bringing them to *double* their 2000 levels. Farmers are now wealthier than ever.

The main drivers of this surge in farm incomes have been the rise in exports and the steep increase in crop prices. Specifically, the ethanol mandate has pushed up the prices not only of corn, but also of crops such as soybeans that have been abandoned by many farmers during the corn gold rush.

Despite the price increases, large subsidies for the five crops mentioned above would continue under the conference agreement. This makes as much sense as subsidizing Silicon Valley businesses during the peak of the dot-com boom. . . .

Subsidizing Millionaires

Currently, all full-time farmers may be eligible for farm subsidies regardless of income (part-time farmers must earn less than $2.5 million annually). President [George W.] Bush reasonably proposed limiting farm subsidies to those who earn less than $200,000 a year.

Rather than follow that commonsense approach, the conference agreement reportedly rejects *all* farmer income tests for the countercyclical and marketing loan subsidy programs and includes only a weak net farm income cap for direct payments ($750,000 for single farmers and $1.5 million for married farmers after all business deductions). Direct payments would also be restricted to singles with *non-farm* incomes under $500,000 ($1 million for married couples).

That is not reform. Farmers with incomes in the millions of dollars would still be eligible for permanent subsidies. Farm subsidies would remain America's largest corporate welfare program: Most subsidies would continue to go to large agribusinesses. President Bush is right to insist that farmers earning more than $200,000 per year no longer be eligible for subsidies.

Key Payment Limits

Currently, farmers face limits of $180,000 apiece in annual commodity payments ($360,000 for those who work on multiple farms and double for married couples). This has created an industry of lawyers who exploit the payment limits' large loopholes. Rather than close the loopholes, the conference agreement reportedly eliminates the payment limits. Specifically, the $75,000 limit for the marketing loan program, which has been subject to the most abuse, would be repealed.

One seemingly positive portion of the farm bill would eliminate the commodity certificates that traditionally have been used to circumvent marketing loan payment limits, but with those limits now gone, farmers would no longer need to use commodity certificates anyway. The conference agreement would wisely eliminate the "three-entity rule" that allows farmers to collect up to $360,000 each year if they work on three or more farms; but, again, with no limit on marketing loan payments, farmers could collect larger subsidies than ever.

The Senate rejected a commonsense proposal by Senators Byron Dorgan (D-ND) and Charles Grassley (R-IA) to limit farm subsidies to $250,000 per farm. In no other profession can employees expect hundreds of thousands of dollars in taxpayer subsidies in both good years and bad. President Bush should insist that such large farm payments are unacceptable

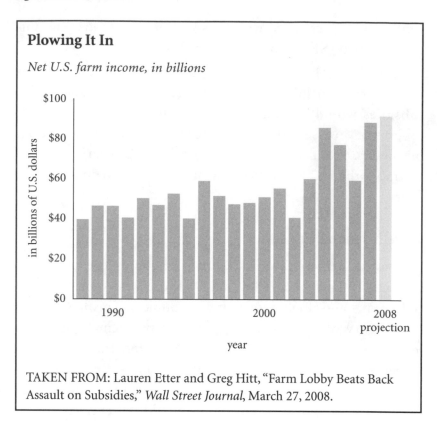

Plowing It In

Net U.S. farm income, in billions

TAKEN FROM: Lauren Etter and Greg Hitt, "Farm Lobby Beats Back Assault on Subsidies," *Wall Street Journal*, March 27, 2008.

for a nation with expensive defense, education, health care, and homeland security priorities.

Increased Spending with Gimmicks

Congress's Pay-As-You-Go (PAYGO) rule requires that entitlement and tax legislation remain deficit-neutral over 10 years. Yet the conference agreement reportedly increases spending by $10 billion over the next decade—plus as much as $10 billion more in gimmicks.

This is no surprise, as the Congressional Budget Office (CBO) identified numerous gimmicks in the original House and Senate bills, such as shifting costs outside the 10-year window and unrealistically assuming that new nutrition and disaster aid provisions will suddenly be eliminated after five years to save money. In addition, conferees violate PAYGO by using the farm spending baseline from 2007, which allows for more spending, rather than 2008.

President Bush proposed a farm bill that would limit spending increase to $5.5 billion and include spending offsets that do not raise taxes. Given record farm incomes and the already bloated federal agriculture budget, even the President's proposal is overly generous. Every dollar of increased farm subsidies must come from (1) other programs such as Social Security, defense, or education; (2) higher taxes; and/or (3) increased debt for future generations. . . .

Increased Subsidy Rates

Despite sky-high crop prices, the conference agreement reportedly raises subsidy rates for more than a dozen crops under the countercyclical and/or marketing loan programs. These programs disburse subsidies whenever crop prices dip below the target prices set in the law. Raising those target prices means that any drop in crop prices would trigger the payment of subsidies sooner and cost taxpayers far more than under current law. The bill also adds four new crops (dry peas, lentils, small chickpeas, and large chickpeas) to the countercyclical program.

These are stealth spending increases, because they do not show up in the CBO cost estimate of the bill. They could also bring a challenge from the World Trade Organization for distorting global trade, potentially leading to retaliation from foreign trading partners that would deplete American exports.

Direct Payments Regardless of Crop Price

No matter how high corn prices soar, the direct payment program would force taxpayers to send $2 billion in direct payments to corn farmers every year. Wheat farmers would receive $1 billion in annual direct payments, and farmers of other crops would receive a combined $2 billion in annual direct payments.

These payments are not based on farmer incomes, crop prices, or any standard of need. Farmers are not even required to grow the listed crop to get a subsidy; the law requires only that they have grown it at some point in the past. There is simply no rationale for these subsidies. Yet the Senate rejected an amendment by Senators Richard Lugar (R-IN) and Frank Lautenberg (D-NJ) that would have redirected these payments into conservation, nutrition, and deficit reduction.

Although prices of the subsidized crops have more than doubled since the last farm bill, the conference agreement reportedly reduces direct payments by just 2 percent, which would then be restored in the final year to preserve the bloated spending baseline. If farm subsidies are designed to compensate farmers for low incomes caused by low crop prices, then continuing to pay more than $5 billion annually to farmers regardless of crop price is an improper use of taxpayer dollars.

Permanent Disaster Aid Program

The conference agreement reportedly spends an additional $3.8 billion over five years to create a permanent farm disaster aid program. Farmers already receive approximately $20 billion in annual commodity and conservation subsidies, plus an additional $3 billion in crop insurance subsidies.

Under this proposal, many farmers who suffer crop losses would automatically collect crop insurance payments *and* disaster payments, essentially double-dipping. This new pot of money would encourage Congress to declare "emergencies" regularly in order to release these funds. Now is it not the time to increase subsidies further.

Modern Farm Policy for the 21st Century

When President Franklin D. Roosevelt introduced farm subsidies in the 1930s, Secretary of Agriculture Henry Wallace called them "a temporary solution to deal with an emergency." That emergency was the collapsing farm incomes that afflicted the 25 percent of the population living on farms. Today, farmers account for just 1 percent of the population, and farm household incomes and net worth are well above the national average, making the original poverty justification obsolete.

In the 21st century, the challenge for farmers is not persistent poverty, but year-to-year income fluctuations brought on by weather- and pest-induced crop unpredictability. The proper response to yearly income fluctuations is not a permanent, massive program of subsidies that farmers receive even in good years. Crop insurance and farmer savings accounts can smooth out the boom and bust years in ways that keep farmers closer to their healthy annual average incomes, all at minimal taxpayer cost. Canada and Australia have already implemented these types of programs.

Additionally, lawmakers must recognize that commodity subsidies distort the farm economy. Farm subsidies induce farmers to grow whatever the government will subsidize, not what consumers want. Stephen Houston, Jr., a Georgia cotton farmer, recently told the *Atlanta Journal-Constitution*, "We're just playing a game. [Market] prices don't have anything to do with what we're doing. We're just looking at the government payments."

Farm policies also harm the environment by promoting overproduction and discouraging crop rotation, violate trade agreements, undercut African farmers, contribute to obesity by subsidizing unhealthy foods, and cost taxpayers and consumers billions of dollars every year.

The agriculture economy has been revolutionized over the past 75 years, and Americans deserve a modern farm bill that reflects today's farm economy. This farm bill clearly fails to meet that standard.

> *"The farm subsidy, he said, is what makes it possible for farmers to make it in more typical years."*

Some U.S. Farmers Say They Need Agricultural Subsidies to Survive

Bruce Hight

In the following viewpoint, Bruce Hight contends that farmers do not see themselves as taking unnecessary money through agricultural subsidies. Farmers claim that they make just enough to get by and that subsidies are there to ensure they can get through bad years. Hight suggests that the American public may misunderstand the true situation of the farmer and the risks they take to produce the food we eat. Bruce Hight is a columnist for the Austin American-Statesman.

As you read, consider the following questions:

1. What other kind of subsidy, besides farm subsidies, is included in the farm bill, according to Hight?

2. What is the "other half of the picture" to farm subsidies identified by the farmer Hight interviewed?

3. What did the farmers Hight talked to say in defense of the subsidies of bigger farms?

Several weeks ago [July 19, 2007], I did a column that irritated, even angered, a bunch of local farmers who receive federal crop subsidies. Only one of these farmers, Steve Raesz, 30, of Taylor, actually contacted me. But with a confident smile, he assured me—and I trust him—that he had heard plenty of his colleagues complain about it. Farmers gripe a lot, he acknowledged, but keep it to themselves.

Various Governmental Subsidies

Briefly, the column noted that Congress was working on a major new farm bill, which it does about every five years. Among many other things, the bill would extend for five years the billions of dollars of taxpayer subsidies given every year to farmers of certain crops, including corn, wheat and cotton. New data available on the Internet shows exactly who gets that taxpayer money and how much, and I reported the top recipients for Travis, Williamson and Hays counties [in Texas]. I also noted how farm industry advocates justify the subsidies, principally on grounds that they keep U.S. food supplies cheap and for national security.

And I reminded readers that the farm bill provides another kind of taxpayer subsidy—food stamps, given to people who need help buying enough food.

Finally, I said a lot of American households (including mine) also take an indirect tax subsidy in the form of a home mortgage interest deduction on our federal income taxes.

The Farmer's Story

A few days after the column ran, Raesz called. Would I come out to listen to a real farmer's side of things? He was working every day from dawn to midnight or later because it's harvest season, he said, but he really wanted to talk.

Farmers in Need

Some farmers certainly would go out of business without Washington's help, and, yes, the rest of us could suffer because we depend upon their crops for food and clothes. A homegrown food supply, even a limited one, is in our national interest. . . .

Limiting subsidies to those who need them . . . can protect our food supply, improve our land and help those farmers who actually deserve it.

William McKenzie,
"How Subsidies Look from the Family Farm,"
Dallas Morning News, *July 31, 2007.*

Of course I said yes, and a rainy day gave him a chance to sleep in before we met at the dinner table in the farmhouse home of his father, Arnold Raesz, 53, and with another Williamson County farmer and friend, Brandon Roznovak, 30, to get their views.

Steve Raesz, a Texas A&M University graduate, said his main objection to the column was that it "led readers to believe we just get lots of free money."

The other half of the picture, he said, is the enormous upfront cost and risk borne by farmers: "What we really make bottom line is not hardly anything. It's just enough to get by.

"Some years the government payment is basically what we make. And then some years, we go in the hole big time. Some years, like this year—good price, good crop—we're going to make a pretty darn good living, some money to put away and things like that."

For this year's corn crop, Raesz said he, his dad and his brother, Shaun, 32, will end up borrowing about $745,000 to rent the land (2,600 acres), plant it, treat it for bugs and plant disease, harvest it and operate and maintain the huge machinery required for the three men to do all that work. There are no other workers—illegal or otherwise—involved, he said. Some years, they have to put out a lot of money to buy a major piece of equipment, such as $110,000 for a used combine.

How much he will make depends on the crop yield, the price he gets for it and his federal subsidy. Last year, he said, he cleared about $17,000. This year, which he said comes along about once every 12 to 15 years (high yield, high price), could bring a profit on corn (including a $36,000 subsidy) of as much as $262,000, with him, his father and brother each getting a third of that, about $87,000.

Earning a Living

The farm subsidy, he said, is what makes it possible for farmers to make it in more typical years.

Roznovak said, "We're just ordinary people. We're not here to be profiteers. We just want to make a living. We don't want a handout." Every year, he said, "you plant for the best and pray that you don't see the worst."

Both Steve and Brandon are single, and Brandon shook his head with a wry smile as he said, "It's hard to find a woman who'll put up with this kind of stuff."

The three men didn't buy my argument that most Americans are quite willing to help true family farmers like themselves through tough years but don't like forking over millions to the biggest farm operations. As they see it, much bigger farms take even bigger risks to produce something the American people must have, and so have earned larger subsidies.

We spent two hours talking, and I enjoyed it. I won't eat crow. But I don't think I'll ever eat corn again without thinking about those Williamson County farmers.

| "Washington simply must stop subsidizing farmers the way it does or risk reversing course on a half-century of steadily expanding trade opportunities."

Agricultural Subsidies Are Not Necessary and Should Be Eliminated

Dean Kleckner

In the following viewpoint, Dean Kleckner argues that the time has come for the United States to begin elimination of agricultural subsidies. He contends that farmers around the world would be better off without subsides. He also claims that successful global trade depends upon the elimination of most subsidies. Dean Kleckner is a farmer and the chairman of Truth About Trade and Technology, a nonprofit group that advocates free trade and biotechnology in agriculture. He was the president of the American Farm Bureau from 1986 to 2000.

As you read, consider the following questions:

1. In what year did New Zealand eliminate all agricultural subsidies?

Dean Kleckner, "Today's Harvest of Shame," *New York Times*, October 15, 2007, p. A21. Copyright © 2007 by The New York Times Company. Reprinted with permission.

2. Why does Kleckner believe that now is an opportune time to change the system by transitioning away from subsidies?

3. How are the European Union's agricultural subsidies less disruptive to international markets, according to the author?

As Congress heads into final negotiations over the farm bill, let's hope our elected officials are paying attention to the headlines: Brazil has scored yet another huge victory at the World Trade Organization [WTO] over America's cotton subsidies; Mexico is likely to file a complaint with the global body over how we subsidize rice farmers; Canada may do the same over corn payments.

This is a troubling pattern, and there's a good chance America will lose more and more cases unless Congress makes changes in the farm bill, which expired last month. [The 2002 Farm Bill expired in September 2007, but it is largely continued by the Food, Conservation, and Energy Act of 2008.] Washington simply must stop subsidizing farmers the way it does or risk reversing course on a half-century of steadily expanding trade opportunities.

Subsidies and Farmers

I know all about subsidies. For years, I took them myself for my corn and soybean farm. I didn't really enjoy it, but they were available and I rationalized my participation: Other industries received payments and tax breaks—why shouldn't I? In addition, I spent 14 years as the head of the American Farm Bureau, the leading farmers' lobby and a prime player in the creation of the subsidy system.

In the 1990s, however, a trip to New Zealand made me realize that eliminating subsidies was not just a free-market fantasy, but rather a policy that could work in an advanced industrial nation. New Zealanders had stopped subsidizing their farmers, cold turkey, in 1984. The transition was controversial and not without its rough spots, yet it succeeded. On that visit and several later ones, I never met a farmer who wanted to go back to subsidies.

Today, it's obvious that we need to transform our public support for farmers. Many of our current subsidies inhibit trade because of their link to commodity prices. By promising to cover losses, the government insulates farmers from market signals that normally would encourage sensible, long-term decisions about what to grow and where to grow it. There's something fundamentally perverse about a system that has farmers hoping for low prices at harvest time—it's like praying for bad weather. But that's precisely what happens, because those low prices mean bigger checks from Washington.

Moreover, these practices hurt poor farmers in the developing world who find themselves struggling to compete. It's one of the reasons that the World Trade Organization won't let these practices stand.

Now would be a particularly opportune time to change the system. Food commodity prices are high, so a transition away from subsidies will hurt farmers less. Today's farmers enjoy much better marketing tools, crop protection and technology than they did only a decade ago.

Subsidies and Global Trade

The alternative is to put off the inevitable and risk a series of trade wars. When the United States loses a WTO case, our aggrieved trading partners gain the right to retaliate through punitive tariffs on many American-made products, not just agriculture. For example, after the trade body ruled against the so-called Byrd amendment of 2000, which mandated that duties charged by Washington on imports deemed to be unfairly priced would go directly to American producers rather

The Harm of Subsidies

The subsidies U.S. cotton farmers receive help destroy any advantage West Africa's farmers have. Since the mid-1990s, when U.S. exports of subsidized cotton began growing—according to Oxfam, U.S. sales went from a low of 17% of the world export market in 1998 to 41% in 2003—the world cotton price has dropped by more than half. The International Cotton Advisory Committee, which promotes cooperation among cotton-producing countries, estimates that developing-world cotton growers, including Burkina Faso, Brazil, India, Mali and Pakistan, have lost $23 billion over the past four years to Western subsidies. The irony, says Oxfam, is that annual losses in export earnings in most West African cotton-producing countries are comparable to U.S. aid donations. Burkina Faso, for instance, received $10 million in U.S. aid in 2002 but lost an estimated $13.7 million in exports because of U.S. cotton subsidies.

Eric Rostan, "The Farm Fight," Time, November 20, 2005.

than to the Treasury, Canada and the European Union slapped sanctions on such imports as American paper, cigarettes and oysters.

Politicians are fond of sticking out their chests and declaring that America's farm policies will be written in Washington, not Geneva. That's a good applause line, but at the same time Congress has rightly determined that it makes sense to participate in a global organization that establishes trade rules. American farmers depend upon the export market. For every two acres of wheat we grow, one is shipped abroad. The last thing we need is for our customers to quit buying because their governments are imposing tariffs with the approval of the World Trade Organization.

Yet Congress is getting in the way. It appears reluctant to approve bilateral agreements with Colombia, Panama and South Korea. With the Doha round of global trade talks having screeched to a halt, these accords are now the primary means for expanding export opportunities.

As for the farm bill, the answer isn't necessarily to get out of the subsidy business entirely (although it's preferable). The WTO permits certain types of subsidies. The European Union spends substantially more public money on farmers per acre than we do, but its methods of payment are more compatible with global rules because they're based on acreage and production history rather than on current crop production and prices. This makes them less disruptive to international markets.

Congress can change the farm bill to meet global rules while serving our public interests of a secure food supply, rural economic development and a cleaner environment. If it doesn't, it will reap us nothing more than a long losing streak at the World Trade Organization.

> "We need agricultural subsidies that support communities instead of supporting commodities."

Agricultural Subsidies Are Needed to Protect Food and Local Communities

Anuradha Mittal

In the following viewpoint, Anuradha Mittal argues that the way agricultural subsidies are used currently is damaging to small farmers around the world. Rather than arguing for the elimination of all subsidies, in support of global trade liberalization, Mittal argues that the way subsidies are used needs to be changed in a manner that will protect agricultural products, local farmers, and local communities. Anuradha Mittal is executive director of the Oakland Institute think tank and an expert on trade, development, human rights, and agricultural issues.

As you read, consider the following questions:

1. According to Mittal, what occupation does the U.S. Department of Labor project to have the largest job loss for the period between 1998 and 2008?

2. What percentage of the world's poor are small-scale and subsistence farmers, according to the author?

3. What does Mittal believe a fair subsidy program would ensure?

The most forceful justification for agricultural subsidies is that they are needed to save small farmers and preserve a way of life. The current agricultural subsidy system in rich countries, however, has only contributed to the decline of the countryside both in the North and the South. There is thus a contradiction between the purpose and consequence of subsidies making it obvious that there is an urgent need to move in a different direction.

The Farmers Subsidies Support

The nearly U.S. $1 billion daily that rich countries spend on subsidies don't go to farmers who resemble John Steinbeck's Joad family [from his novel *Grapes of Wrath*]. Far from benefiting small farmers, subsidies go overwhelmingly to large, capital-intensive agriculture as support is closely linked with production levels and land ownership. Most family farms get nothing but a tax bill.

In the United States, family farmers have been sold out to corporate agribusiness with ever-increasing numbers of farm bankruptcies and foreclosures reaping a grim harvest of suicides, alcoholism, and a loss of community. Subsidizing well-heeled agribusiness interests has ensured the continued exodus of independent family farmers from the land. In the 1930s, 25% of the U.S. population lived on the nation's 6 million farms. Today America's 2 million farms are home to less than 2% of the population. The U.S. Department of Labor projects that the largest job loss among all occupations between 1998–2008 will be in agriculture. This is not surprising when the average farm-operator household earns only 14% of its income from the farm and rest from off-farm employment. A

New York Times article in 2002 reported, "The biggest economic collapse is happening in counties most tied to agriculture, in spite of the subsidies." Out of the poorest 50 counties in the United States, 49 are rural counties.

In France, subsidies are skewed toward the rich farmers as well, with 15% of farms receiving in excess of 20,000 euros accounting for 60% of total payments. At the same time, the peasant population has declined by one third, with the number of suicides in the French countryside increasing rapidly.

Effect on the World Market

This agricultural system robs not just the family farmers in rich countries but the world's poor. Today rich countries like the United States are bound under the Agreement on Agriculture (AOA) of the World Trade Organization (WTO) obligations to commit to reducing domestic and export subsidies, increasing market access, and governing agriculture trade with more rigorous disciplines on domestic farm policies. However, the federal government has been doling out an average of $11.3 billion annually between 1995 and 2004. More than 90% goes to producers of corn, cotton, wheat, rice, and soybeans, with just 10% of farms receiving 74% of these subsidies. These five crops are dramatically overproduced and sell on global markets at below the cost of production, depressing the global commodity prices of crops that developing countries count on while wiping out poor farmers and enriching transnational food-industry giants.

The numbers are alarming. The United States provides 200 times more support in hidden export support than it declares, equivalent to $6.6 billion a year. The U.S. export price of wheat in 1995 was 23% below the U.S. cost of production; by 2001 the export price was 44% below the cost of production. In cotton, despite its higher production costs, the United States increased its world market share even when world prices fell to 38 cents a pound in May 2002. Africa lost about $300 million, with Mali and Benin losing more than their aid receipts from the United States, and Burkina Faso losing more than what it got in Heavily Indebted Poor Countries (HIPC) debt relief. In 2003, around 28,000 U.S. cotton farmers received $2.4 billion, 13 times more than the entire GDP of Burkina Faso, a country where more than two million people depend on cotton production for their living. The result is a reverse Robin Hood effect: robbing the world's poor to enrich American agribusiness.

Agriculture is the source of livelihood for over 40% of people on earth. Most of these producers are small-scale and subsistence farmers who constitute 75% of the world's poor. This fact lends strategic urgency to the need to change an agricultural subsidy system in the North that shores up an unjust and unsustainable corporate controlled industrial food system.

The Truth About Free Trade

First we need to dismantle one of the great myths that free trade helps farmers and the poor. It does not! Attempts to leave farmers at the mercy of the free market only hasten their demise. The focus on export crops for trade has meant increasing yields, with farmers becoming dependent on chemical inputs. Many have stopped rotating their crops, instead devoting every acre to corn, wheat, or some other commodity crop and creating vast monocultures that require still more chemicals to be sustained. This has destroyed our biodiversity. Vast industrial farms require costly equipment for planting and harvesting, increasing the capital intensity of agriculture. As costs rise, prices fall in markets flush with surplus. As prices fall, farmers need subsidies, which are available to big growers and agribusiness only. Land values and cash rents increase. This encourages heavy borrowing. Rich landowners get richer and young farmers cannot afford to get started. An agricultural bubble economy is created. Inevitably it crashes as

A Concern About Free Trade

Trade is not a panacea for poverty alleviation or for development more generally. It is important not to overstate the possible gains from the Doha Round [of World Trade Organization negotiations], as has been done by many political leaders, commentators, and activists. For example, it has been fashionable to state that trade can do more than development aid to lift people out of poverty in developing countries. Though this may be theoretically true, it is clear that trade has a modest contribution to make and is only one policy mechanism among many that must be pursued to achieve economic growth and rising incomes.

An unrealistic expectation of gains is not harmless. It can lead to pressure for inappropriate policies and could create a bandwagon effect where the very legitimate defensive concerns of developing countries are ignored to achieve illusory gains. Errors in analysis can lead to increases in poverty, not the hoped-for reductions, in developing countries. For the poorest countries, where there is little margin for error, the risks are particularly acute.

Sandra Polaski, "Winners and Losers:
Impact of the Doha Round on Developing Countries,"
Carnegie Endowment, *March 2006,*
www.carnegieendowment.org.

subsidies fail to keep pace with falling crop prices. Farms go bankrupt. Free trade in agriculture starves our farmers.

Our right to food has been undermined by dependence on the vagaries of the free market promoted by the international financial institutions. Instead of ensuring the right to food for all, these institutions have created a system that prioritizes export-oriented production and has increased global hunger and poverty while alienating millions from productive resources such as land, water, and seeds. The "world market" of agricultural products simply does not exist. What exists is an international trade of surpluses in grain, cereals, and meat dumped primarily by the EU [European Union], the United States, and members of the Cairns Group. Behind the faces of trade negotiators are powerful transnational corporations such as Cargill and Monsanto, which are the real beneficiaries of domestic subsidies and international trade agreements. Fundamental change in this repressive trade regime is essential.

Not surprisingly then, farmers organizations and social movements around the world have denounced the liberalization of farm products promoted by the WTO and other regional and bilateral free trade agreements. Instead of trade, small farmers movements prioritize healthy, good quality, and culturally appropriate subsistence production for the domestic market and for the sub-regional or regional markets. These farmers' priority is to produce for their families and communities, then to seek access to the domestic market before seeking to export.

Resisting Trade Liberalization

The Doha Round of the WTO will mean certain death for untold numbers of farmers who will face increased competition from foreign subsidized products when their agricultural tariffs are reduced. If this terrible situation occurs, the developing countries should be able to defend themselves by not reducing their tariffs on food products and products of their small farmers, and should be provided a Special Safeguard Mechanism, a tool that allows developing countries to work against the practice of dumping that is killing peasants. Under this mechanism, a developing country can raise the tariffs on a product if there is an import surge of the product. And they should be able to choose for themselves the Special Products (SP) that are exempted from obligations of tariffs and domestic subsidies. In essence, designating products as SP means taking them out of the WTO. In addition the developing countries should also be able to revert to the use of quantitative restrictions, which they had given up in false expectation that the Northern countries would stop their protection. In the wake of WTO talks stalled at the mini-ministerial in June 2006, farmers groups worldwide, including the Asian Peasant Coalition, have already declared that all products are special products! This buffer would at least allow countries to protect their most sensitive sectors from tariff reductions, and therefore protect millions of farmers' lives.

Some Subsidies Needed

Agriculture and food are fundamental to the well-being of all people, both in terms of access to safe and nutritious food and as foundations of healthy communities, cultures, and environment. To ensure this we need agricultural subsidies that support communities instead of supporting commodities. Instead of production- and price-linked subsidies, a fair subsidy system would ensure small farmers access to local markets, fair prices for their products, and, when necessary, credit and technical assistance. Such a system would support the development of cooperatives and promote the consumption and production of local crops raised by small, sustainable farms. It would ensure farmers' rights to land, seeds, and water; support conservation practices; and protect indigenous rights.

In short, this is about ensuring a new system of agricultural trade that would guarantee food sovereignty; the right of people and countries to define their own agricultural and food policies according to the needs and the priorities of local communities, including mechanisms to protect domestic food production; ensure strict control of food imports to stabilize internal market prices; and supply management systems to avoid dumping on the world markets.

> *"The nation's agricultural policies oper-*
> *ate at cross-purposes with its public-*
> *health objectives."*

To Ensure Quality Food, Current Agricultural Subsidies Need to Be Eliminated

Michael Pollan

In the following viewpoint, Michael Pollan argues that American agricultural policy, which includes subsidies, is responsible for the fact that unhealthy food is cheaper than healthy food. This, in turn, contributes to social problems such as obesity. Pollan claims that the farm bill needs to be considered a food bill, and eliminating subsidies is one step toward changing the way Americans eat. Michael Pollan is a contributing writer to the New York Times Magazine *and is the Knight Professor of Journalism at the University of California, Berkeley. Pollan is author of* In Defense of Food: An Eater's Manifesto, *and* The Omnivore's Dilemma.

Michael Pollan, "You Are What You Grow," *New York Times Magazine*, April 22, 2007, pp. 15–18. Reprinted by permission of International Creative Management, Inc. Copyright © 2007 by Michael Pollan for The *New York Times*.

As you read, consider the following questions:

1. What three subsidized foods are the key ingredients in Twinkies, according to Pollan?

2. What agricultural trend does Pollan claim is inextricably linked with the trend of high immigration levels from Mexico into the United States?

3. In addition to agricultural subsidies, what other fact about modern agriculture needs to be addressed within a food bill, as Pollan envisions it?

A few years ago, an obesity researcher at the University of Washington named Adam Drewnowski ventured into the supermarket to solve a mystery. He wanted to figure out why it is that the most reliable predictor of obesity in America today is a person's wealth. For most of history, after all, the poor have typically suffered from a shortage of calories, not a surfeit. So how is it that today the people with the least amount of money to spend on food are the ones most likely to be overweight?

The Cost of Calories

Drewnowski gave himself a hypothetical dollar to spend, using it to purchase as many calories as he possibly could. He discovered that he could buy the most calories per dollar in the middle aisles of the supermarket, among the towering canyons of processed food and soft drink. (In the typical American supermarket, the fresh foods—dairy, meat, fish and produce—line the perimeter walls, while the imperishable packaged goods dominate the center.) Drewnowski found that a dollar could buy 1,200 calories of cookies or potato chips but only 250 calories of carrots. Looking for something to wash down those chips, he discovered that his dollar bought 875 calories of soda but only 170 calories of orange juice.

As a rule, processed foods are more "energy dense" than fresh foods: they contain less water and fiber but more added

165

fat and sugar, which makes them both less filling and more fattening. These particular calories also happen to be the least healthful ones in the marketplace, which is why we call the foods that contain them "junk." Drewnowski concluded that the rules of the food game in America are organized in such a way that if you are eating on a budget, the most rational economic strategy is to eat badly—and get fat.

This perverse state of affairs is not, as you might think, the inevitable result of the free market. Compared with a bunch of carrots, a package of Twinkies, to take one iconic processed food-like substance as an example, is a highly complicated, high-tech piece of manufacture, involving no fewer than 39 ingredients, many themselves elaborately manufactured, as well as the packaging and a hefty marketing budget. So how can the supermarket possibly sell a pair of these synthetic cream-filled pseudocakes for less than a bunch of roots?

Agricultural Policy and Health

For the answer, you need look no farther than the farm bill. This resolutely unglamorous and head-hurtingly complicated piece of legislation, which comes around roughly every five years and is about to do so again [in 2007], sets the rules for the American food system—indeed, to a considerable extent, for the world's food system. Among other things, it determines which crops will be subsidized and which will not, and in the case of the carrot and the Twinkie, the farm bill as currently written offers a lot more support to the cake than to the root. Like most processed foods, the Twinkie is basically a clever arrangement of carbohydrates and fats teased out of corn, soybeans and wheat—three of the five commodity crops that the farm bill supports, to the tune of some $25 billion a year. (Rice and cotton are the others.) For the last several decades—indeed, for about as long as the American waistline has been ballooning—U.S. agricultural policy has been designed in such a way as to promote the overproduction of these five commodities, especially corn and soy.

That's because the current farm bill helps commodity farmers by cutting them a check based on how many bushels they can grow, rather than, say, by supporting prices and limiting production, as farm bills once did. The result? A food system awash in added sugars (derived from corn) and added fats (derived mainly from soy), as well as dirt-cheap meat and milk (derived from both). By comparison, the farm bill does almost nothing to support farmers growing fresh produce. A result of these policy choices is on stark display in your supermarket, where the real price of fruits and vegetables between 1985 and 2000 increased by nearly 40 percent while the real price of soft drinks (aka liquid corn) declined by 23 percent. The reason the least healthful calories in the supermarket are the cheapest is that those are the ones the farm bill encourages farmers to grow.

A public-health researcher from Mars might legitimately wonder why a nation faced with what its surgeon general [Richard Carmona] has called "an epidemic" of obesity would at the same time be in the business of subsidizing the production of high-fructose corn syrup. But such is the perversity of the farm bill: the nation's agricultural policies operate at cross-purposes with its public-health objectives. And the subsidies are only part of the problem. The farm bill helps determine what sort of food your children will have for lunch in school tomorrow. The school-lunch program began at a time when the public-health problem of America's children was undernourishment, so feeding surplus agricultural commodities to kids seemed like a win-win strategy. Today the problem is overnutrition, but a school lunch lady trying to prepare healthful fresh food is apt to get dinged by USDA [U.S. Department of Agriculture] inspectors for failing to serve *enough* calories; if she dishes up a lunch that includes chicken nuggets and Tater Tots, however, the inspector smiles and the reimbursements flow. The farm bill essentially treats our children as a human Disposall for all the unhealthful calories that the farm bill has encouraged American farmers to overproduce.

The Influence of the Farm Bill

To speak of the farm bill's influence on the American food system does not begin to describe its full impact—on the environment, on global poverty, even on immigration. By making it possible for American farmers to sell their crops abroad for considerably less than it costs to grow them, the farm bill helps determine the price of corn in Mexico and the price of cotton in Nigeria and therefore whether farmers in those places will survive or be forced off the land, to migrate to the cities—or to the United States. The flow of immigrants north from Mexico since NAFTA [North American Free Trade Agreement] is inextricably linked to the flow of American corn in the opposite direction, a flood of subsidized grain that the Mexican government estimates has thrown two million Mexican farmers and other agricultural workers off the land since the mid-90s. (More recently, the ethanol boom has led to a spike in corn prices that has left that country reeling from soaring tortilla prices; linking its corn economy to ours has been an unalloyed disaster for Mexico's eaters as well as its farmers.) You can't fully comprehend the pressures driving immigration without comprehending what U.S. agricultural policy is doing to rural agriculture in Mexico.

And though we don't ordinarily think of the farm bill in these terms, few pieces of legislation have as profound an impact on the American landscape and environment. Americans may tell themselves they don't have a national land-use policy, that the market by and large decides what happens on private property in America, but that's not exactly true. The smorgasbord of incentives and disincentives built into the farm bill helps decide what happens on nearly half of the private land in America: whether it will be farmed or left wild, whether it

How Cheap Commodities Connect to Cheap Food

Beginning in the 1970s, food manufacturers recognized the cheap costs of commodity "inputs" and began to find enterprising ways to use them in their food products. Around the same time that prices were dropping for corn, Japanese food scientists figured out how to process corn into high fructose corn syrup (HFCS), a product that could be used to sweeten food in place of sugar. HFCS, a liquid, was easier to work with than sugar and also had the added benefits of being six times sweeter than sugar, prolonging shelf life, resisting freezer burn and making food look as if it had been browned in an oven. But best of all, because it was made from corn, it was cheap.

Soybeans, too, yielded a cheap and highly useful food product: vegetable oil. Oils are an important part of the human diet, but nutritionists have found that different oils have very different effects on the body. Much of the vegetable oil in the United States is altered in an industrial process called partial hydrogenation. This process makes an oil more solid, provides longer shelf life in baked products, increases fry-life for cooking oils and produces a desirable texture. Unfortunately, partial hydrogenation also creates trans fatty acids, recognized as the unhealthiest type of fat. Like HCFS, trans fats have become ubiquitous in processed foods, from fast food to breakfast cereals to crackers to baked goods.

Heather Schoonover and Mark Muller,
"Food Without Thought: How U.S. Farm Policy Contributes
to Obesity," Institute for Agriculture and Trade Policy,
March 2006, www.iatp.org.

will be managed to maximize productivity (and therefore doused with chemicals) or to promote environmental stewardship. The health of the American soil, the purity of its water, the biodiversity and the very look of its landscape owe in no small part to impenetrable titles, programs and formulae buried deep in the farm bill.

Given all this, you would think the farm-bill debate would engage the nation's political passions every five years, but that hasn't been the case. If the quintennial antidrama of the "farm bill debate" holds true to form this year [2007], a handful of farm-state legislators will thrash out the mind-numbing details behind closed doors, with virtually nobody else, either in Congress or in the media, paying much attention. Why? Because most of us assume that, true to its name, the farm bill is about "farming," an increasingly quaint activity that involves no one we know and in which few of us think we have a stake. This leaves our own representatives free to ignore the farm bill, to treat it as a parochial piece of legislation affecting a handful of their Midwestern colleagues. Since we aren't paying attention, they pay no political price for trading, or even selling, their farm-bill votes. The fact that the bill is deeply encrusted with incomprehensible jargon and prehensile programs dating back to the 1930s makes it almost impossible for the average legislator to understand the bill should he or she try to, much less the average citizen. It's doubtful this is an accident.

A Food Bill

But there are signs this year [2007] will be different. The public-health community has come to recognize it can't hope to address obesity and diabetes without addressing the farm bill. The environmental community recognizes that as long as we have a farm bill that promotes chemical and feedlot agriculture, clean water will remain a pipe dream. The development community has woken up to the fact that global poverty can't be fought without confronting the ways the farm bill depresses world crop prices. They got a boost from a 2004 ruling by the World Trade Organization that U.S. cotton subsidies are illegal; most observers think that challenges to similar subsidies for corn, soy, wheat or rice would also prevail.

And then there are the eaters, people like you and me, increasingly concerned, if not restive, about the quality of the food on offer in America. A grass-roots social movement is gathering around food issues today, and while it is still somewhat inchoate, the manifestations are everywhere: in local efforts to get vending machines out of the schools and to improve school lunch; in local campaigns to fight feedlots and to force food companies to better the lives of animals in agriculture; in the spectacular growth of the market for organic food and the revival of local food systems. In great and growing numbers, people are voting with their forks for a different sort of food system. But as powerful as the food consumer is—it was that consumer, after all, who built a $15 billion organic-food industry and more than doubled the number of farmer's markets in the last few years—voting with our forks can advance reform only so far. It can't, for example, change the fact that the system is rigged to make the most unhealthful calories in the marketplace the only ones the poor can afford. To change that, people will have to vote with their votes as well—which is to say, they will have to wade into the muddy political waters of agricultural policy.

Doing so starts with the recognition that the "farm bill" is a misnomer, in truth, it is a *food* bill and so needs to be rewritten with the interests of eaters placed first. Yes, there are eaters who think it in their interest that food just be as cheap as possible, no matter how poor the quality. But there are many more who recognize the real cost of artificially cheap food—to their health, to the land, to the animals, to the public purse. At a minimum, these eaters want a bill that aligns agricultural policy with our public-health and environmental values, one with incentives to produce food cleanly, sustainably and humanely. Eaters want a bill that makes the most healthful calories in the supermarket competitive with the least healthful ones. Eaters want a bill that feeds schoolchildren fresh food from local farms rather than processed surplus commodities from far away. Enlightened eaters also recognize their dependence on farmers, which is why they would support a bill that guarantees the people who raise our food not subsidies but fair prices. Why? Because they prefer to live in a country that can still produce its own food and doesn't hurt the world's farmers by dumping its surplus crops on their markets.

The devil is in the details, no doubt. Simply eliminating support for farmers won't solve these problems; overproduction has afflicted agriculture since long before modern subsidies. It will take some imaginative policy making to figure out how to encourage farmers to focus on taking care of the land rather than all-out production, on growing real food for eaters rather than industrial raw materials for food processors and on rebuilding local food economies, which the current farm bill hobbles. But the guiding principle behind an eater's farm bill could not be more straightforward: it's one that changes the rules of the game so as to promote the quality of our food (and farming) over and above its quantity.

Such changes are radical only by the standards of past farm bills, which have faithfully reflected the priorities of the agribusiness interests that wrote them. One of these years, the eaters of America are going to demand a place at the table, and we will have the political debate over food policy we need and deserve. This could prove to be that year: the year when the farm bill became a food bill, and the eaters at last had their say.

| "Almost all the emphasis is on cutting subsidies, as if government subsidies are the only thing standing between farmers and markets that deliver fair prices."

To End Global Poverty, It Is Not Enough to Eliminate Agricultural Subsidies

Sophia Murphy

In the following viewpoint, Sophia Murphy contends that the proposals to come out of the trade talks within the World Trade Organization (WTO) are not doing enough to help the most disadvantaged countries achieve development goals. Murphy claims that the focus on ending subsidies is misguided, as she believes eliminating subsidies will not solve the problems currently facing people in the developing world. Sophia Murphy is senior advisor on trade issues for the Institute for Agriculture and Trade Policy, where her work focuses on agricultural trade rules, U.S. trade and agricultural policy, and the interests of developing countries.

Sophia Murphy, "Will the Doha Round Play a Role in Ending Global Poverty?" *Au Courant*, vol. 13, Spring 2005, pp. 7–9. Copyright © 2009 Canadian Council for International Co-operation. Reproduced by permission.

As you read, consider the following questions:

1. Murphy notes that the UN Food and Agriculture Organization reported that the number of hungry people in the world grew by how many between 2000 and 2004?

2. What does the author state is the worst problem that the proposed rules in the July Package fail to address?

3. What three areas do trade rules need to address in order to end poverty, according to the author?

As civil society organizations from around the globe unite to call for action against poverty, government trade officials are immersed in negotiations to establish the next "round" of multilateral trade rules. It is a crucial year to drive home the message that trade rules must support poverty eradication.

Development Disappears from View

Global trade negotiations take place within the framework of the Doha Agenda. This agenda for negotiations was adopted by trade ministers in November 2001, at the fourth World Trade Organization (WTO) Ministerial Conference in Doha, Qatar.

Trade officials promoted the Doha Agenda as the launch of a "Development" round. But the name was clearly a misnomer. Against developing country wishes, rich countries were determined to launch a wide trade round. They pushed hard at Doha for agreement to negotiate a broad agenda, including "new issues" such as investment and competition, which were opposed by developing countries. In the last hours of the Doha meeting, developed countries succeeded in getting the new issues into the agenda. To push forward unpopular measures, they also managed to link all the issues into a single round, so that countries could not agree to negotiate some aspects and opt out of others. In exchange, developing countries were promised consideration of a mounting backlog of trade "implementation problems", and help for their trade policy-related needs.

Some three years later [2004] with the adoption of the July Package, any "development" aspect of the agenda has disappeared from view, leaving WTO business as usual in its wake. *Not a single one* of the more than 80 implementation issues raised by developing countries has been addressed. Rich countries are pouring aid into trade capacity-building programs, but these programs have been widely criticized for failing to take a sufficiently broad look at trade and its role in development policy. The only other sign that rich countries have any intention of helping developing countries is their agreement in the July Package—after a long and bitter fight—to drop investment, competition, and transparency in government procurement as issues in this round.

Little else in the July Package reflects just and sustainable trade priorities. The agenda is still very broad, and includes services, industrial tariffs, agriculture, trade facilitation and more. The July Package calls for an accelerated timetable for countries to list service sectors for liberalization. The pressure on the South to commercialize services raises significant development concerns about poor people's access to essential services such as water, health care and education.

On industrial tariffs, the July Package repeats proposals that were made in Cancun [2003] (and strongly rejected by developing countries). These proposals to lower tariffs for industrial products will favour companies that are already established in the international marketplace. Most developing country firms are unlikely to be able to hold their own against such global competitors. The proposals will do nothing to help least-developed and otherwise disadvantaged countries diversify and strengthen their industrial base.

Ending Global Poverty

If the world community takes seriously the goal of halving global poverty by [2015], trade will be only a tiny part of the solution.

To have any meaningful impact, rich countries would have to make good on their commitment to, as the Doha Declaration states, place developing countries' "needs and interests at the heart of the Work Programme adopted in this declaration." That would mean recognizing in practice the need for "special and differentiated treatment" for developing countries, to leave them the policy tools to industrialize and develop. It would mean accepting developing-country proposals to let countries exempt sensitive food crops such as rice, maize, and wheat from liberalization.

Timothy A. Wise, "The WTO's Development Crumbs,"
Foreign Policy in Focus, *January 23, 2006, www.fpif.org.*

Little Progress on Agriculture

Some of the biggest concerns with the July Package relate to agriculture. Agriculture is the main source of employment and livelihood for people in many developing countries, and is arguably the most important sector for an agenda to eradicate poverty. Concerns about agriculture were a main cause of the breakdown in talks at Cancun.

The need for new rules is clear. Global trade in agriculture is a mess: the current mix of national policies and multilateral rules has sent commodity prices plunging and dramatically increased poverty. Farmers around the world are leaving their land, unable to make a living growing food. Food security (the ability of countries to feed themselves with adequate and culturally appropriate food, whether from their own production, imports or some mixture of the two) seems a more elusive goal than ever. The UN [United Nations] Food and Agriculture Organization reported in December 2004 that the number of hungry people had grown by 18 million since 2000, so there are now 852 million people living with hunger. Governments are a long way from achieving the Millennium Development Goal of halving the number of hungry people by 2015.

Many, including the WTO, blame the agricultural policies of rich countries for the devastation of rural communities in developing countries. In particular, rich countries are criticized for subsidizing domestic production, which is said to create surplus production that is dumped on world markets, which in turn undercuts developing country producers.

There is a lot to change in rich-country agricultural policies, but the July Package does not get at the problem. Rich countries have again ensured that the proposed rules will not force any actual cuts to their spending on agriculture. The *scope* for spending will be diminished, but spending *levels* will remain largely unchanged.

The Role of Subsidies

A deeper problem is that almost all the emphasis is on cutting subsidies, as if government subsidies are the only thing standing between farmers and markets that deliver fair prices. The WTO rules focus on domestic support, tariffs, and export subsidies. The working assumption is that government's role in agriculture should be minimized and the private sector should be left unregulated. As a result, the proposed rules fail to address one of the worst problems: the dumping of agricultural products in world markets at prices that are below the cost of production.

Subsidies are part of the problem. But dumping is also a *structural* feature of current commodity markets because of the power of a small number of private firms. Huge firms control the sale of chemicals and seeds to farmers, grain purchasing and processing, livestock production, and the sale of food and other products to consumers. Their market power enables them to set prices at the expense of farmers and consumers alike. For example, firms sell US cotton in world markets at prices close to 50 percent below what it costs to produce. That cotton drives down the world price for cotton, at the expense of growers in some of the world's poorest countries, including Burkina Faso and Mali.

More fundamentally, the WTO approach fails to respect the broader objectives that many countries have for agriculture—including meeting the human right to food and establishing a strong rural sector as a basis for economic development. Both of these objectives depend on a strong government role and on regulating the private sector.

Time for Trade Justice

How could the Doha Round support an agenda to end poverty? Trade rules need to: allow policy space so countries can determine the best course for their specific development needs; end dumping; and permit policies that strengthen farmers' power in the marketplace.

Developing countries need policy space to determine what will work best for their needs. To protect their development interests, countries need to maintain control of their economies. For different countries, and for different sectors within a country, more than one approach to trade rules is needed. Flexibility is key.

Opening markets can be an important tool for a country, as when newly opened markets helped Bangladesh avoid famine after the rice harvest failed in 1998. But governments may also need to restrict imports, or manage them, to protect other interests. State trading enterprises may offer services that the private sector is unable or unwilling to provide. Restricting imports may be necessary to protect rural livelihoods and to stabilize domestic prices.

Global agricultural trade rules must outlaw dumping. To address dumping, much greater transparency in commodity markets is needed, including information on companies' market shares. We need a standard measurement for production costs that is made publicly available. The right of developing countries to block dumped produce at their borders needs to be protected.

Periodical Bibliography

The following articles have been selected to supplement the diverse views presented in this chapter.

Sylvain Charlebois and Wolfgang Langenbacher — "Subsidies Are Not the Answer: Farmers Need to See Themselves as Part of the Agricultural Industry, with a Viable New Business Model to Boot," *Globe & Mail*, April 25, 2006.

Helena Cobban — "Time to End U.S. Cotton Subsidies," *Christian Science Monitor*, March 20, 2005.

Thomas G. Donlan — "Stop Feeding the Farmers: Agriculture Ought to Be Treated Like Any Other Business," *Barron's*, November 12, 2007.

Economist — "The Farmer's Friend," November 5, 2005.

Chris Edwards and Tad DeHaven — "Save the Farms—End the Subsidies," *Washington Post*, March 3, 2002.

Victor Davis Hanson — "Harvesting Money in a Hungry World," *New York Times*, August 1, 2008.

Blair Hull — "Farm Subsidies and Other Sacred Cows: It's Time for Slaughter," *Crain's Chicago Business*, January 5, 2009.

Paul Krugman — "Grains Gone Wild," *New York Times*, April 7, 2008.

Lawrence Lessig — "A Modest Proposal: Hold Hollywood Hostage Till We Kill Farm Subsidies," *Wired Magazine*, January 2004.

Dan Morgan, Sarah Cohen, and Gilbert M. Gaul — "Growers Reap Benefits Even in Good Years," *Washington Post*, July 3, 2006.

Tom Tancredo — "Farm Bill Shamelessly Buries Taxpayers," *Denver Post*, May 29, 2008.

Washington Post — "The Charm of the Farm," October 19, 2005.

OPPOSING
VIEWPOINTS®
SERIES

CHAPTER 4

What Are Some Alternatives to Agricultural Subsidies?

Chapter Preface

On the one hand, agricultural subsidies as currently utilized are charged with the overproduction of unhealthy foods, environmental degradation from the overproduction of certain crops, distortion of crop prices that harms farmers in the developing world, and a harmful increase in corporate farming, among other things. On the other hand, concerns about the complete elimination of agricultural subsidies include worries about adequate national internal food supply, concern about farmers' livelihoods, and fears of the loss of significant cultural practices associated with agriculture. This has caused many to look at ways to both eliminate certain effects of current subsidy practices that are seen as harmful while finding alternatives to safeguard national food security, farmer livelihood, and cultural practices. One movement gaining hold in both developing and developed nations is a focus on sustainable, local farming practices.

According to the U.S. Department of Agriculture (USDA), the number of operating farmers markets in the United States has more than doubled from 1,755 in 1994 to 4,684 in 2008. Farmers markets allow consumers to buy locally grown, often organic, farm-fresh produce. The direct marketing from farmer to consumer allows the farmer to keep more of his or her proceeds, cultivating loyalty directly between grower and consumer. Farmers markets also promote better nutrition with consumers having access to fresh, in-season produce, frequently grown without pesticides. A related movement gaining ground is the community supported agriculture (CSA) movement, which involves members purchasing a share of a farmer's harvest, thus supporting farmers by assuming the costs and risks of farming while also taking advantage of quality produce below retail prices. The growth of farmers markets and the CSA movement in the United States is one proposed local solution to both the concerns about agricultural subsidies and the concerns associated with eliminating agricultural subsidies.

The current debate about agricultural subsidies within the World Trade Organization (WTO) Doha Development Round focuses on the elimination of trade barriers, including agricultural subsidies. The goal of trade liberalization is to open markets to farmers all around the world to trade their agricultural products freely and fairly. The local food movement embodied by the farmers markets and CSA movement offers an alternative to further globalization of the agriculture system. Whether such a solution can work throughout the globe remains to be seen. It is one proposed solution to the concerns related to the current agricultural practices, with or without agricultural subsidies. This and other solutions are discussed in this chapter.

| "Nation states are well advised to have some form of food security objective and policies."

Internal Food Security Is Needed to Deal with the Global Food Crisis

Thomas Dobbs

In the following viewpoint, Thomas Dobbs argues that the rise in food commodity prices is the latest crisis that shows a need to reform agricultural policy in a way that involves both more reliance and less reliance on the free market. Dobbs believes that while commodity subsidies should be abandoned as part of having more reliance on markets, it is also necessary for nation states to have less reliance on markets by creating internal food security policies. Thomas Dobbs is professor emeritus of economics at South Dakota State University and a W.K. Kellogg Foundation Food & Society Policy Fellow.

As you read, consider the following questions:

1. By what percentage have food commodity prices risen between 2006 and 2008, according to Dobbs?

2. According to the author, what modern myth about free trade needs to be dismantled in favor of less reliance on markets?

3. The author claims that nation states need to work more on developing food security policy that incorporates what two elements?

I made several trips to India and Pakistan between the late-1960s and the early-1980s. The 'Green Revolution' was just emerging during my first trip in 1967–68, when I spent 6 months collecting agricultural data for my Ph.D. dissertation near Allahabad, on the fertile Gangetic Plain of northern India. I later lived for 1-1/2 years in Pakistan during the mid-1970s, as an agricultural economist with the U.S. Agency for International Development. By the time of my stay in Pakistan, the Green Revolution pace of change in the subcontinent had begun to slow. During and immediately following my various trips, I was always struck by the contrast between the prevailing U.S. view of 'markets' and the views of Indian and Pakistani governments. It seemed to me that India and Pakistan needed to place more reliance on markets and the U.S. needed more regulation of markets.

The Food Crisis

Now, some 40 years after the Green Revolution erupted in Asia and some other parts of the developing world, we again appear to be facing the kind of world food crisis that India faced just prior to that revolution. Food commodity prices have risen by more than 60 percent in the last 2 years [2006–2008], to their highest levels in decades. A constellation of factors have brought about the pressures on food supplies and consequent increase in prices, including crop failures in some parts of the world, the surge in biofuels production and associated use of cropland for fuel rather than food, continued growth in the world's population, higher energy prices, and rising incomes in developing countries—which induce diet changes that put more pressure on grain supplies. Moreover, annual worldwide growth in agricultural output has been much slower in the last two decades than in the previous two decades following the Green Revolution. Between 1970 and 1990, world grain and oilseed production increased at an annual average rate of 2.0 percent per year, while world population growth averaged 1.7 percent annually. Population growth was lower between 1990 and 2007, averaging 1.4 percent annually. However, growth in grain and oilseed production averaged only 1.3 percent per year in the later period.

Food scarcity and associate price increases always hit the poor hardest. As a consequence, in recent months [January–February 2008], we have seen food riots, government limitations or increased taxes on food exports by the governments of some exporting countries, and a variety of short-term national and international responses to get affordable food in the hands of the poor in many developing countries.

Suggested Solutions

We are also seeing an intense discussion of what kinds of national and international agricultural and food policies are needed to deal with this food crisis on a long-term basis.

Pascal Lamy, the Director General of the World Trade Organization (WTO), for example, recently stated that successful resolution of the WTO's Doha Round of trade negotiations could help provide medium- to long-term solutions to the world food problem. In his May 7 [2008] report to the WTO General Council, he stated:

> WTO deal could help soften the impact of high prices by tackling the systematic distortions in the international market for food. We all aim to substantially lower barriers to trade in agricultural products and diminish levels of trade distorting subsidies, particularly in developed countries that

have hampered food production and investment in agriculture in many developing countries.

Bob Davis, writing May 12 [2008] in the *Wall Street Journal* Online, stated that the current world food crisis represents a breakdown in the global agricultural market. "Skyrocketing prices should boost production of grain, which can be shipped around the world. But not if countries hoard supplies and restrict exports." He went on to describe efforts by the World Bank and International Monetary Fund (IMF) to persuade national governments not to restrict food commodity exports.

Likewise, the May 11 [2008] *Washington Post* Editorial Page called for the U.S. to use "strong diplomacy" in attempting to persuade national governments not to restrict food commodity exports.

These, in effect, are all calls for more reliance on 'markets'. More reliance on markets does, indeed, constitute part of the needed long-term response. But we need to avoid a mentality that markets by themselves will deliver long-term solutions to the food crisis. In reality, we need both 'more' and 'less' reliance on markets.

More Reliance on Markets

First, how do we need more reliance on markets? We do not need a narrow WTO view of 'free markets' for agriculture—which in fact do not prevail in the globalized agriculture system and are unlikely ever to prevail so long as national governments are responsive to felt needs of their citizens for food security. But WTO advocates are correct in calling for the European Union (EU) and the U.S. to dismantle the forms of farm subsidy that until recently have resulted in 'dumping' and associated depressed farm prices in developing countries, thereby undermining incentives to expand agricultural production within those countries themselves. The U.S. has 'talked the talk' of free trade in WTO negotiations, but has consistently failed to 'walk the walk'. We need a lot more reliance on

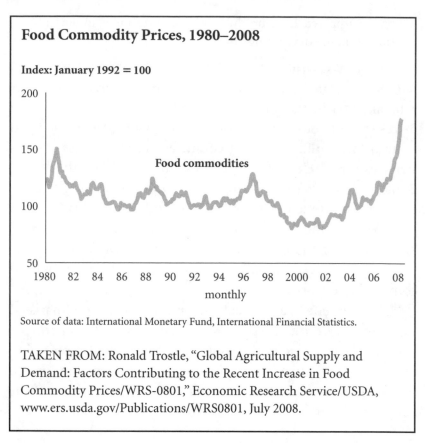

Food Commodity Prices, 1980–2008

Index: January 1992 = 100

Food commodities

monthly

Source of data: International Monetary Fund, International Financial Statistics.

TAKEN FROM: Ronald Trostle, "Global Agricultural Supply and Demand: Factors Contributing to the Recent Increase in Food Commodity Prices/WRS-0801," Economic Research Service/USDA, www.ers.usda.gov/Publications/WRS0801, July 2008.

true market forces in the U.S. agricultural sector, rather than heavy reliance on artificial markets created by commodity subsidies, highly subsidized crop and farm revenue insurance, taxpayer-funded disaster programs that encourage production that is ecologically and economically inappropriate to some regions, and ethanol subsidies and mandates.

Greater reliance on true market forces in the U.S. would not only be beneficial to farmers and the poor in developing countries, it would also be beneficial to the long-run sustainability of our own agricultural resources. The artificial markets we have created since World War II in this country have resulted in chemical-intensive crop production practices, loss of biodiversity, and large-scale livestock confinement systems—all of which 'externalize' many of the true costs of food production and undermine our production capacity for the long run. Greater U.S. reliance on markets also would, over time, lead to production and consumption of healthier foods, especially of fruits and vegetables and of food consumed closer to where it is grown.

Less Reliance on Markets

Second, how do we need less reliance on markets in addressing the food crisis on a long-term basis? We can start by dismantling the modern myth that free trade carried out globally in accordance with WTO rules would eliminate the need for nation states to have any internal food security. What kind of fantasy world is that? Western Europe was absolutely committed to food security following the devastating effects of two twentieth century world wars, and food security was the critical objective in formation of the EU's Common Agricultural Policy. Is it any wonder that the EU has been reluctant in WTO negotiations to adopt the U.S. view that food security is unimportant? If we needed any further reminder that food security within nation states will always be the number one agricultural priority, witness the food riots and resultant controls on exports referred to previously in this article! Deep down, we know that the U.S. also would somehow limit exports if we were faced with the kinds of shortages occurring now in some other parts of the world.

It is all well and good for WTO, World Bank, and IMF officials to urge countries not to limit their food commodity exports, but it is naïve to build long-term policies on the assumption that nation states will not behave in this way. Therefore, nation states are well advised to have some form of food security objective and policies, though this sometimes can be done by a collection of well-integrated nations, as in the case of the EU.

Food Security

One element of food security would be a sensible grain reserve policy, something the U.S. no longer has. The U.S. dismantled its long-standing grain reserve policies some years ago. I distinctly recall conversations at the time with economics colleagues who contended this was a good thing, that 'the market' could take care of whatever reserves 'the market' needed. Government grain reserves sometimes were managed for political purposes (true enough), and were best done away with, ran the argument. I expressed skepticism about reliance on 'the market' for strategic and price-stabilizing reserves. Unfortunately, I believe recent events have proven me to be correct. The fact that government controlled grain reserves are not always managed as they should be is not sufficient reason to abandon them. Far better to make reserve programs function as they should.

A second element of food security is for nations—both 'advanced' and 'developing'—to place new or renewed emphasis on agricultural output growth through ecologically integrated, *sustainable* approaches. While not completely abandoning comparative advantage principles and agricultural trade, this approach recognizes that most nations of any significant size need to have some internal food production capacity. Producing a portion of the food supply domestically and sustainability helps satisfy food security needs and is the best way to have many poor people involved in agriculture, both as farmers and consumers of affordable, nutritious food.

Governments have a legitimate role in supplementing and regulating the market to promote sustainable food production. They can supplement the market through support for research, technical assistance, funding for infrastructure, creation of a positive climate for emergence of social capital, and cost-share assistance for conversion to ecological farming systems. They can regulate the market by enforcing tough environmental standards to curb polluting and unsustainable farming practices, thereby creating a more level playing field for ecologically sustainable systems.

Have my views on markets fundamentally changed since those early years of observing differences of emphasis between the U.S. and the Indian subcontinent? I don't think so, though I hope I am always learning and refining my policy views. I have always been an economic pragmatist, and wary of sweeping economic ideologies. Clearly, markets have their place, and in some ways we need more reliance on market forces and institutions to deal with the food crisis that confronts us. But in other ways we need less reliance, or at least more regulations and more policies and programs to supplement the market.

> "Cultivating local control begins with solidifying basic rights: rights to land and water and rights to political and social capital for marginalized communities."

Agricultural Policies Need to Support Local Control

Corrina Steward

In the following viewpoint, Corrina Steward contends that agricultural policy reform should focus on more than the elimination of subsidies. She believes that the view that privileges local control over corporate control, and uses the rights-based principle of food sovereignty, is beginning to change the language of agricultural trade for the better. Corrina Steward is a resource rights specialist at Grassroots International, a human rights and international development organization that supports community-led sustainable development projects.

As you read, consider the following questions:

1. According to Steward, what percentage of food is produced for local consumption and never traded on the global market?

Corrina Steward, "Farming for Families and Food, Not Corporate Profits," *Foreign Policy in Focus*, April 19, 2005, pp. 1–3. Copyright © 2005 IRC and IPS. www.fpic.org. All rights reserved. Reproduced by permission.

2. Agricultural subsidies perpetuate a vicious cycle of poverty and resource degradation through what five effects, according to the author?

3. With food sovereignty, the poverty and resource degradation cycle can be controlled by what three policies, according to the National Family Farmer Coalition (NFFC)?

Two contradictory visions of globalization are sweeping around the world: one favors a top-down model of economic development via militaristic, corporate aggression. The other favors grassroots-led, democratic pluralism and seeks to produce diverse local development models suited to the needs of local communities.

The Two Views

Proof of these inconsistencies abounds. Paul Wolfowitz's election to the presidency of the World Bank [in 2005; he resigned in 2007] signifies the advancement of a militaristic approach to controlling global resources; at the same time, thousands around the world continue to protest against the war in Iraq and other examples of U.S. imperialism. Schemes to privatize water, agricultural crops, and other life-giving resources continue to be pushed through proposed trade agreements and state-corporate relationships; yet, global social movements are calling for community sovereignty with unprecedented forcefulness and international solidarity.

One of the biggest ironies is that global agricultural production is regulated by international trade rules when nearly 90% of food is produced for local consumption and never traded on the global market. José Bové, a leader of the international farmers' movement Via Campesina, points out, "No one would have believed [before the World Trade Organization came into existence] that we would get to the point where the biggest social movement in the world is a farmers' movement."

It is indeed surprising that agriculture—the most rudimentary form of industrial capitalism—is at the center of trade conflicts during this advanced stage of global industrialization. Yet, it also indicates a huge misunderstanding by free marketers of the local realities in the agricultural regions of the developing world, and even in U.S. and European farming communities.

Trade Rules Ignore Dumping

The World Trade Organization's (WTO) Agreement on Agriculture (AoA) focuses on market access, export subsidies, and domestic support as a means for implementing a fair trading system. Reform in these areas focuses on export-oriented farming, which receives the majority of government support, and does not guarantee improved livelihoods for the farmers producing for non-export markets or on a small scale.

The WTO measures overlook several practices and trends, including the key issues of dumping of over-produced commodities and corporate control of the agricultural market.

A recent Institute for Agriculture and Trade Policy report pointed out that dumping is a human rights issue: "Coupled with the lack of social safety nets, [dumping] has caused serious human rights concerns since the implementation of the AoA, particularly for small-scale farmers who lose their livelihoods due to competition from subsidized, dumped imports." The human rights argument goes even further. Not only does dumping eliminate economic opportunities for rural communities, it denies local farmers the social and cultural values of their farming practices.

Trade Rules Ignore Corporate Control

Corporate control of agricultural markets is intricately linked to government subsidies and also has human rights implications. In February [2005], the [George W.] Bush administration proposed reducing the annual ceiling on payments to U.S. farmers from $360,000 to $250,000. George Naylor, president of the National Family Farmer Coalition (NFFC), argues that this would pit U.S. cotton and rice producers against other U.S. commodity producers because the caps would only affect the former.

Rather than allow a rift between U.S. commodity producers, Naylor insists, "Farmers have got to get together to say 'this is ridiculous.' We're destroying our communities, our resources, all for the benefit of a few corporations. This policy is not good for us, for the United States. It's only good for those few corporations."

Corporate agribusinesses are the main profiteers of subsidies as they provide the means for keeping production costs low. Subsidies perpetuate a vicious cycle of poverty and resource degradation by encouraging overproduction of crops, soil erosion, increased pesticide use, below-cost prices, and deflated farmer income. Agribusiness benefits from subsidies through the lowering of crop prices, which minimizes their costs and increases their profits.

"The same forces that are working against farmers in Africa and El Salvador are working against farmers in Iowa," Naylor concludes. Due to the poverty and resource degradation cycle, producers are forced to take whatever price commodity buyers offer—limiting farmers' capacity to define their livelihoods.

Rights-Based Food Sovereignty

As trade agreements seek to homogenize global agriculture policies and production, Via Campesina—a global network of farmers with as many as 200 million members—is calling for

Food Sovereignty

La Via Campesina promotes the idea of "food sovereignty" as an answer to the concept of food security that created more hunger in the world and more poverty among farm families. Food sovereignty is an alternative concept that supports the people in their struggle against neoliberal and liberal policies such as those that are imposed by the international financial institutions, the WTO, and the transnational agribusiness corporations through free trade and the liberalization of agriculture.

Food sovereignty is a people's right to nutritional and culturally appropriate foods that are accessible, produced in a sustainable and ecological way and their right to decide on their own food and production system. This concept places those who produce, distribute, and consume foods at the heart of the systems and food policies above the demands of the markets and corporations. It offers us a strategy to resist and dismantle free and corporate trade and the current food regime and to orient food, farm, grazing, and artisanal fishing systems to prioritize local economies and local and national markets. It grants power to peasants and family farmers, to artisanal fishermen and to traditional shepherds, and places food production, distribution, and consumption on the bases of sustainability of the social and economic environment. Food sovereignty ensures that the rights to access and manage our land, our territories, our water, our seeds, our animals and biodiversity are in the hands of those who produce food. . . .

La Via Campesina, "Fifth International Conference of La Via Campesina: Press Kit," 2008, www.viacampesina.org.

local policies and diversified production models. They are making farming communities' needs central to agricultural policies and providing a much-needed reality check to U.S. and European Union trade negotiators.

Via Campesina has begun to carve out a new policy space in global agricultural politics for "food sovereignty." The concept of food sovereignty is gaining political and social leverage as proposals like the Free Trade Area of the Americas (FTAA) and the Central American Free Trade Agreement (CAFTA) continue to threaten the ability of family farmers in both the North and the South to determine how food will be produced and who will make food production decisions. Via Campesina's members believe in "the peoples', Countries', or State Unions' RIGHT (sic) to define their agricultural and food policy, without any dumping vis-à-vis third countries."

Inserting food sovereignty into current agricultural trade and policy debates reframes them to approach national resources from a human rights approach rather than an economic one. The human right to essential resources is not a new concept. Several United Nations treaties already recognize the right to food, and traditional community rights over biodiversity are supported by the UN Convention on Biological Diversity.

With food sovereignty, the rights-based approach to international dialogue has resulted in new alliances between the global North and South, such as the alliance between U.S. farmer groups like the NFFC and peasant farming organizations in Central and South America. The food sovereignty fight is a multinational farmers' struggle against corporate agribusiness and the national and international policies that support them.

Beyond Subsidies

Rather than focusing on limiting subsidies, NFFC explains that the poverty and resource degradation cycle could be controlled by:

1. Increasing global commodity prices through price supports;

2. Maintaining reserves of excess production to be used in times of need (e.g., drought) and as a means of maintaining steady commodity prices; and

3. Stopping production of a given commodity when there is an oversupply.

To implement these measures requires the right to prevent foreign imports from flooding national and local agricultural markets and reigning in corporate influence on the market. Cultivating local control begins with solidifying basic rights: rights to land and water and rights to political and social capital for marginalized communities.

Despite the refusal of U.S. leadership to acknowledge that democratic, grassroots approaches to development are popularly supported world-wide, this model is gaining considerable ground. Every day, the Landless Peoples' Movement in Brazil gains access to land necessary for community self-sufficiency and demonstrates that local control of vital resources is more environmentally and economically sustainable. Other movements—from local food networks in the U.S., to cross-border agro-ecological collaborations in Central America—are formulating their own community-based development models.

Via Campesina is changing the language of agricultural trade from a language of corporatization to a language of farmers' rights and local sovereignty. This resistance to corporate agriculture is the basis of hope for rural communities around the world.

| "A better safety net will do far less to amplify problems caused by agricultural production than current farm policy does."

Safety Nets Are a Better Alternative to Agricultural Subsidies

Britt Lundgren

In the following viewpoint, Britt Lundgren argues that ending agricultural subsidies is not the answer to solving all environmental problems caused by agriculture, but she does believe that the system can be changed to operate as a better safety net. Lundgren believes an insurance program could save money while helping farmers in actual need, and also help to solve some of the problems caused by current agricultural policy. Britt Lundgren is an agricultural policy fellow in the Land, Water and Wildlife Program of the Environmental Defense Fund, a nonprofit organization that works to find solutions to environmental problems.

As you read, consider the following questions:

1. According to Lundgren, the current structure of farm subsidies sends what message to farmers?

2. The Lugar-Lautenberg Amendment proposed to replace the current subsidy system with what, according to the author?

3. In what three ways does the author believe that the Lugar-Lautenberg plan could make headway toward solving environmental problems tied to agriculture?

Fixing farm policy, which has been the single largest influence on the shape of agriculture in the U.S. since the Dust Bowl, is not easy. "Not easy" will seem a drastic understatement to anyone who has followed the endless debate on the Senate floor over the past two weeks [November 5–16, 2007] which has produced much hand-wringing and rhetoric about our "safe and abundant food supply," but no actual Farm Bill.

Tom Philpott has argued in recent posts that farm subsidies are a symptom of the problems associated with modern agriculture rather than the cause, and that efforts to end subsidies are bad policy. In his view, overproduction is the true culprit, and unless farm bill reforms include a mechanism to control supply we will continue to have problems.

It's easy to blame everything on overproduction, but it is just not accurate. Prices for corn, soybeans, and many other commodity crops are higher than they've ever been right now. Prices don't rise when there's too much of a commodity, they rise when demand exceeds supply.

Ending Subsidies Not the Solution

I do agree with Mr. Philpott on one point: simply ending farm subsidies is not going to immediately end all of the environmental problems caused or aggravated by agricultural production.

But farm subsidy reform advocates are not talking about ending subsidies. We don't want to pull the rug out from underneath farmers. Instead, we want to exchange the wall-to-wall shag carpet for something more modest—a safety net for farmers that is less market-distorting and costs less than $9 billion a year. A better safety net will do far less to amplify problems caused by agricultural production than current farm policy does, and will also free up funds that can be used to address these problems.

The current structure of farm subsidies sends a message to farmers: no matter what happens with the weather or the market, you will continue to get a check from Uncle Sam. Regardless of whether there's a bumper crop and the market is flooded, or there has been hail or drought or floods and there's practically nothing in the field to harvest, you will get these checks.

Prices are high right now—it's not at all accurate to say that subsidies are causing overproduction. But if the ethanol boom tanks, which could easily happen in the near future, the current structure of farm subsidies would insulate farmers from market signals telling them to plant less. At that point, subsidies would continue to prop up production levels, and thus would contribute to overproduction.

The Lugar-Lautenberg Proposal

As I explained in a recent post, Senators Richard Lugar (R-Ind.) and Frank Lautenberg (D-N.J.) have an amendment [the Lugar-Lautenberg Amendment was defeated in the U.S. Senate on December 11, 2007] to the Senate Agriculture Committee's Farm Bill that is a promising—and much less expensive—alternative to the current subsidy system. It would replace the current system with a county—based revenue insurance program. Revenue insurance would cost much less than the current subsidy system, and the savings generated would be reinvested in a wide array of programs, many of which help

The Lugar-Lautenberg Amendment

There has never been a better time for farmers to change. Thanks to strong foreign and domestic demand for energy crops, net farm income is forecast to be $87 billion [in 2007] up $28 billion from 2006 and $30 billion above the average for the previous ten years and setting a new record for new farm income.

As a result, average farm household income is projected to be almost $87,000 in 2007, up 8 percent from 2006, 15 percent above the five-year average between 2002 and 2006, and well above median U.S. household income. Farm revenue may be high today, but this will not always be the case. It is critical that we have an appropriate safety-net in place to assist these farmers during times of need.

Agriculture policy is too important for rural America and the economic and budgetary health of our country to continue the current misguided path. Our amendment provides a much more equitable approach, produces higher net farm income for farmers, increases farm exports, avoids stimulating over-production, and gives more emphasis to environmental, nutritional, energy security and research concerns. More importantly, this proposal will protect the family farmer through a strong safety-net and encourage rural development in a fiscally responsible and trade compliant manner.

Senator Richard G. Lugar,
Senate floor speech, December 11, 2007,
http://lugar.senate.gov.

address the ills that Philpott blames on overproduction. The amendment would spend an additional:

- $1.2 billion conservation programs for working farm, ranch, and forestland;

- $200 million for the Seniors Farmers' Market Nutrition Program;

- $200 million for the WIC Farmers' Market Nutrition Program;

- $20 million for the Farmers Market Promotion Program;

- $75 million for socially disadvantaged farmers and ranchers;

- $70 million for research and marketing development for fruits and vegetables.

The insurance program would be available to all types of farmers, not just producers of a few commodity crops, and as Philpott himself points out, payouts would be based on revenues, which are largely tied to the size of a farm. Counties with more agricultural production would still get more money than counties with less agricultural production when revenues fall, because more farmers from the first group of counties would make claims. But this is a far better alternative than the way funds are distributed under current policies, which heavily favor the largest producers of just a few types of row crops.

Farmers in the urban periphery or other areas where people are trying to revive local food systems would be equally eligible to participate in this insurance program—something that isn't a realistic option for most of them now unless they're growing one of the major commodity crops. As agricultural revenues in these counties grow, these farms would be eligible for more support from the federal government. And in the meantime, they would benefit from increased funding for farmers markets, conservation, and specialty crops provided by the Lugar-Lautenberg amendment.

The environmental problems tied to agriculture are going to take a long time to solve, no matter what. But the Lugar-Lautenberg amendment would bring us a lot closer to our goal. It would eliminate extra incentives for producers to plant more crops when prices are low, increase funding for the conservation programs that help farmers reverse the environmental damage of agriculture, and create incentives for farmers to be better stewards of their land. It would be a vast improvement over the current system, and it deserves the support of Congress and the American public.

"They should divert these resources to funding the World Program and help the really poor battle today's hunger crisis."

Instead of Funding Agricultural Subsidies, Resources Should Be Used for World Hunger

Kamal Nath

In the following viewpoint, Kamal Nath argues that farm subsidies in the United States and the European Union are to blame for a host of problems. Nath believes the food crisis is exacerbated by shifted production of agricultural products, the West's pursuit of ethanol, and the cheap subsidized exports coming out of America and Europe—all of which he contends are the result of subsidies. Kamal Nath is India's minister for commerce and industry within the department of commerce.

As you read, consider the following questions:

1. According to Nath, agricultural subsidies provided by the United States and the European Union to their farmers shift production in what way?

Kamal Nath, "Farm Subsidies Are the Real Culprit," *Business Week Online*, May 14, 2008. Copyright © 2008 by McGraw-Hill, Inc. Reproduced by special permission.

2. Why is there a hunger crisis in West Africa, according to the author?

3. According to the author, what has always provided a solution to food crises?

For more than half a century, developed countries in the West have systematically and egregiously distorted the global production and trade of agricultural commodities through an elaborate range of domestic and export subsidies. It is naive to believe that distortions perpetuated for so long will now be swept under the carpet using the excuse of "the hunger crisis." Let's get some facts straight.

First, it is indisputable that the lavish farm subsidies provided by the U.S. and the European Union to their farmers distort global production and trade. These subsidies artificially depress prices, encourage inefficient producers (in the U.S. and EU) and discourage competitive producers (in the developing countries). Just look at the impact of subsidies on cotton. Some of the most competitive producers are countries in West Africa. They receive a pittance as the price for cotton because of the huge subsidies to a handful of farmers in the U.S. And exactly the same argument holds good for a host of other agricultural commodities—rice, wheat, soybeans, corn, pulses, sugar, dairy products, and so on. The bottom line: Subsidies shift production away from efficient developing countries to inefficient developed countries.

Second, the U.N. is now clearly saying that the ethanol/biofuel policies aggressively pursued by developed counties have exacerbated the current food crisis. Huge subsidies are being handed out to encourage production of biofuels by converting food products into energy products. This is what is responsible for drastically increasing prices of goods such as corn. So, what are these policies achieving? Developed countries subsidize their inefficient farmers, and the corn grown is then used to produce subsidized biofuels, which makes energy

prices cheaper. The net result, to let the rich drive their cars and SUVs cheaply! And, who pays the real price for this? The world at large.

Rice From Overseas

Third, if rice can be efficiently grown in many parts of West Africa, why is there a hunger crisis? Well, developed countries sell cheap rice to these countries (cheap only because of the extensive subsidies). West African countries, therefore, import their food rather than grow it. And, in a year when there is a sudden supply shock (as is the case today), food prices suddenly escalate, and these countries face a crisis because they can't afford the imported food. Are the developed countries' subsidies blameless? No!

The point is that whether we look at the current crisis or the one that has been perpetuated for the past 50 years, ultimately the blame rests at the door of the developed world and the policies they have aggressively pursued. Surely, it is time to put a stop to this. We need to solve this once and for all rather than trying to "compromise" and duck making a decision.

Notwithstanding Malthusian doomsday predictions and the economic logic of Engel's Law, the world has quite happily managed its food situation. Yes, we do have a crisis today. But it is not one that cannot be managed. Prophets of doom, ascribing a looming crisis to demographics or changes in consumption because of rising incomes, have been belied time and again. How? Technology has always provided a solution. We had our Green Revolution, as did other parts of the world. It is now time to invest resources into R&D and technology to engineer another Green Revolution. That is the way forward. This is most certainly not the time to continue perpetuating intrinsically and fatally flawed policies. Let the developed countries abandon their farm subsidies. Instead, they should divert these resources to funding the World Food Program and help the really poor battle today's hunger crisis.

Periodical Bibliography

The following articles have been selected to supplement the diverse views presented in this chapter.

Alan Beattie	"Sweetheart Deals," *Financial Times*, July 26, 2008.
David Bennett	"Growers, Economists Push for Grain Reserves," *Southeast Farm Press*, August 5, 2008.
Christian Science Monitor	"Farmers Deserve Better," November 1, 2007.
Chuck Conner	"Farmers Deserve Better," *Washington Times*, November 19, 2007.
Daniel G. De La Torre Ugarte and Alejandro Dellachiesa	"The Limits of Trade Liberalization in Agriculture and the Search for an Alternative Framework to Benefit Countries in the South," Agricultural Policy Analysis Center (APAC), November 2005. www.agpolicy.org.
Kent Garber	"At Last, Some Respect for Fruits and Veggies," *U.S. News & World Report*, March 24, 2008.
Sam Hurst	"Betting the Farm," *Gourmet*, April 2008.
Sebastian Mallaby	"Rice and Baloney: Irrational Policies the World Over Are Making the Food Crisis Worse," *Washington Post*, May 19, 2008.
New York Times	"A Surer Way to Feed the Hungry," August 4, 2007.
Daryll E. Ray and Harwood D. Schaffer	"Targeting Policy Toward Each of Three Agricultures," Agricultural Policy Analysis Center (APAC), November 2004. www.agpolicy.org.
David G. Victor	"Putting Rich Farmers First," *Newsweek*, July 14, 2008.

For Further Discussion

Chapter 1

1. According to Daryll E. Ray, Daniel G. De La Torre Ugarte, and Kelly J. Tiller, subsidies increased drastically in the late 1990s because of depressed crop prices. Thus, in their view, eliminating subsidies will not solve the problem of the low prices that create a need for subsidies. How does Chris Edwards disagree with this account of the relationship between subsidies and low crop prices?

Chapter 2

1. Claire Godfrey, for Oxfam, argues that agricultural subsidies lead to the dumping of agricultural products in developing countries at prices below the costs of production. Sophia Murphy, Ben Lilliston, and Mary Beth Lake argue that this dumping of cheap agricultural products is not the result of agricultural subsidies, but the result of what? What further information would you need to determine who is correct?

2. Per Pinstrup-Andersen argues that agricultural subsidies in rich countries are harming poor people in the developing world and making rural development difficult. Arvind Panagariya disagrees, claiming that the least developed countries benefit from the low import prices created by agricultural subsidies. Though they differ on this point, on what point do they both agree with respect to agricultural trade liberalization?

3. Amy Frykholm claims that agricultural subsidies in the United States lead to poor nutrition and health problems such as obesity because of the focus on five key crops, while the *Washington Times* claims that worldwide high

food prices arc partially the result of agricultural subsidies. How might it be argued that growing more diverse crops and ending agricultural subsidies could worsen the global food shortage crisis?

Chapter 3

1. In the viewpoint of Daniel Griswold, Stephen Slivinski, and Christopher Preble, as well as the viewpoint of Tom Philpott, the problem of overproduction of certain crops leading to environmental degradation is discussed. Griswold, Slivinski, and Preble believe that ending subsidies will halt this degradation, whereas Philpott believes it will continue even if the agricultural subsidies are stopped. What is the crux of their disagreement on this point?

2. Brian M. Riedl claims that farmers today are wealthier than ever thanks to agricultural subsidies. This claim contradicts those of the farmers who spoke with Bruce Hight, who claim that the subsidies are necessary for them to survive. Based on what the farmers told Hight, what might they say to Riedl to explain why the statistics on farm income from 2002 to 2008 do not give an accurate picture of their need for subsidies?

3. Dean Kleckner argues for the elimination of agricultural subsidies, whereas Anuradha Mittal argues for a change in the way subsidies are used, opting for subsidies that support communities instead of commodities. How do you think Kleckner would respond to Mittal's suggestion of supporting food sovereignty?

4. Both Michael Pollan and Sophia Murphy argue in favor of agricultural policy that supports local food production and control (for different reasons). Give one reason for and one reason against allowing local control of agricultural policy.

Chapter 4

1. Thomas Dobbs argues that it is a myth that free trade will eliminate the need for nations to have policies that support internal food security. Nonetheless, Dobbs believes that subsidies should be abandoned in favor of more reliance on the free market, while at the same time making room for internal food security policies. How does Corrina Steward go further than Dobbs in arguing against reliance on global controls?

2. Both Britt Lundgren and Kamal Nath argue that the money spent on current agricultural subsidies should be revised. How do they differ with respect to where each believes the money ought to be redirected?

Organizations to Contact

The editors have compiled the following list of organizations concerned with the issues debated in this book. The descriptions are derived from materials provided by the organizations. All have publications or information available for interested readers. The list was compiled on the date of publication of the present volume; the information provided here may change. Be aware that many organizations take several weeks or longer to respond to inquiries, so allow as much time as possible.

Agricultural Policy Analysis Center (APAC)
The University of Tennessee, 310 Morgan Hall
Knoxville, Tennessee   37996-4519
(865) 974-7407 • fax (865) 974-7298
e-mail: mlwilson@utk.edu
Web site: www.agpolicy.org

APAC aims to provide information on agricultural, environmental, and macroeconomic policies and regulations. APAC examines policies, regulations, and conditions that affect how farmers operate their business and how the agriculture sector performs. The center publishes several newsletters and a weekly agricultural policy column, and it provides access to center presentations, all available at its Web site.

American Farm Bureau Federation (AFBF)
600 Maryland Ave. SW, Suite 1000W, Washington, DC   20024
(202) 406-3600 • fax (202) 406-3602
e-mail: webmaster@fb.org
Web site: www.fb.org

AFBF is an independent organization governed by and representing farm and ranch families, with the goal of enhancing and strengthening the lives of rural Americans, and building strong, prosperous agricultural communities. The AFBF works as a grassroots organization at all levels to analyze problems and formulate action to achieve educational improvement, economic opportunity, and social advancement, and to promote the national well-being. The AFBF has a variety of publications available at its Web site, including "A Consumer Guide to the Farm Bill."

Environmental Working Group (EWG)
1436 U Street NW, Suite 100, Washington, DC   20009
(202) 667-6982
Web site: www.ewg.org

The mission of the EWG is to use the power of public information to protect public health and the environment. EWG provides practical information to consumers and pushes for policy changes in areas such as government subsidies. Various research publications and other research tools on the topic of farm subsidies are available at EWG's Web site, including a farm subsidy database.

Farm Aid
11 Ward Street, Suite 200, Somerville, MA   02143
(800) FARM-AID • fax (617) 354-6992
e-mail: info@farmaid.org
Web site: www.farmaid.org

Farm Aid is a nonprofit organization whose mission is to keep family farmers on their land by raising awareness through an annual concert and year-round campaign. Farm Aid works to promote food from family farms, grow the Good Food Movement, help farm families in crisis, and bolster family-farm centered agriculture. A variety of information is available at Farm Aid's Web site, including access to its monthly newsletter.

Institute for Agriculture and Trade Policy (IATP)
2105 First Ave. S, Minneapolis, MN   55404
(612) 870-0453 • fax (612) 870-4846

e-mail: iatp@iatp.org
Web site: www.iatp.org

IATP works with organizations around the world to analyze how global trade agreements affect domestic farm and food policies. IATP advocates for fair trade policies that promote strong health standards, labor and human rights, the environment, and, most fundamentally, democratic institutions. The institute publishes a variety of reports available at its Web site, including "A Fair Farm Bill for Public Health."

Institute for Food and Development Policy—Food First
398 60th Street, Oakland, CA   94618
(510) 654-4400 • fax (510) 654-4551
e-mail: info@foodfirst.org
Web site: www.foodfirst.org

The purpose of the Institute for Food and Development Policy, Food First, is to eliminate the injustices that cause hunger. Some of the institute's programs include assisting with the building of local agri-foods systems; accompanying farmers forging food sovereignty; and supporting groups struggling to democratize development including land, resources, and markets. The institute has a variety of books, fact sheets, backgrounders, and policy briefs available at its Web site, including "Policy Brief No. 16: The World Food Crisis—What's Behind It and What We Can Do About It."

International Forum on Globalization (IFG)
1009 General Kennedy Avenue #2, San Francisco, CA   94129
(415) 561-7650 • fax (415) 561-7651
e-mail: ifg@ifg.org
Web site: www.ifg.org

IFG promotes equitable, democratic, and ecologically sustainable economies in the era of globalization. IFG produces numerous publications; organizes high-profile, large public events; hosts issue-specific seminars; coordinates press conferences and media interviews at international events; and participates in other activities that focus on the myriad consequences of globalization. Among its publications is "The Rise and Predictable Fall of Globalized Industrial Agriculture."

Organization for Competitive Markets (OCM)
P.O. Box 6486, Lincoln, NE 68506
Web site: www.competitivemarkets.com

OCM is a nonprofit, public policy research organization with the purpose of returning the food and agriculture sector to true supply–demand based competition. OCM undertakes an extensive communications program to distribute knowledge and information about free market principles in the American tradition. The organization publishes a monthly newsletter, among other publications, on the topic of antitrust and trade policy in agriculture.

Oxfam International
226 Causeway Street, 5th Floor, Boston, MA 02114-2206
(800) 77-OXFAM • fax (617) 728-2594
e-mail: info@oxfamamerica.org
Web site: www.oxfam.org

Oxfam International is a confederation of organizations working to end poverty and injustice. Oxfam's agriculture campaign seeks to raise awareness about issues in agriculture, including the issue of biofuels and the issue of rising food prices. Oxfam publishes numerous reports, including "A Billion Hungry People: Governments and Aid Agencies Must Rise to the Challenge."

World Trade Organization (WTO)
Centre William Rappard, Rue de Lausanne 154
Geneva 21 CH-1211
Switzerland
(41-22) 739 51 11 • fax (41-22) 731 42 06
e-mail: enquiries@wto.org
Web site: www.wto.org

The WTO is the only global international organization dealing with the rules of trade between nations, with the goal of helping producers of goods and services, exporters, and importers conduct their business. The WTO sponsors trade agreements between member nations and supports trade liberalization, in particular supporting the reduction of agricultural subsidies. Among the information available at its Web site is "Agriculture: Fairer Markets for Farmers."

Worldwatch Institute

Worldwatch Institute, 1776 Massachusetts Ave. NW
Washington, D.C. 20036
(202) 452-1999 • fax (202) 296-7365
e-mail: worldwatch@worldwatch.org
Web site: www.worldwatch.org

The Worldwatch Institute's mission is to generate and promote insights and ideas that empower decision makers to build an ecologically sustainable society that meets human needs. The Worldwatch Institute's Sustainable Agriculture Program aims to create a roadmap for farmers, agribusiness, and other agricultural decision makers toward a system that meets global food needs, protects natural resources, and reduces rural poverty. The institute publishes *World Watch* magazine, numerous reports, and books, including *Eat Here: Reclaiming Homegrown Pleasures in a Global Supermarket.*

Bibliography of Books

Kym Anderson and Will Martin — *Agricultural Trade Reform and the Doha Development Agenda.* Washington, DC: World Bank Publications, 2005.

Kym Anderson, Ernesto Valenzuela, and Will Martin — *The Relative Importance of Global Agricultural Subsidies and Market Access.* Washington, DC: World Bank Publications, 2006.

Kym Anderson and Johan Swinnen, eds. — *Distortions to Agricultural Incentives in Europe's Transition Economies.* Washington, DC: World Bank Publications, 2008.

Neil Andrews, David Bailey, and Ivan Roberts — *Agriculture in the Doha Round.* London: Commonwealth Secretariat, 2004.

John Baffes and Harry De Gorter — *Disciplining Agricultural Support Through Decoupling.* Washington, DC: World Bank Publications, 2005.

Francois Bourguignon and Luiz A. Pereira da Silva, eds. — *The Impact of Economic Policies on Poverty and Income Distribution: Evaluation Techniques and Tools.* New York: Oxford University Press/World Bank Publications, 2003.

José Bové and Francois Dufour — *Food for the Future: Agriculture for a Global Age.* Malden, MA: Polity Press, 2005.

W.R. Cline — *Trade Policy and Poverty.* Washington, DC: Institute for International Economics, 2004.

Guillermo de la Dehesa — *Winners and Losers in Globalization.* Malden, MA: Blackwell, 2006.

Ashok Gulati and Sudha Narayanan — *The Subsidy Syndrome in Indian Agriculture.* New York: Oxford University Press, 2003.

Thomas W. Hertel and L. Alan Winters, eds. — *Poverty and the WTO: Impacts of the Doha Development Agenda.* New York: Palgrave Macmillan/World Bank Publications, 2006.

Daniel Imhoff — *Foodfight: The Citizen's Guide to a Food and Farm Bill.* Healdsburg, CA: Watershed Media, 2007.

David Cay Johnston — *Free Lunch: How the Wealthiest Americans Enrich Themselves at Government Expense (and Stick You with the Bill).* New York: Portfolio, 2007.

Timothy Josling, Donna Roberts, and David Orden — *Food Regulation and Trade: Toward a Safe and Open Global System.* Washington, DC: Institute for International Economics, 2004.

Won W. Koo and P. Lynn Kennedy — *International Trade and Agriculture.* Malden, MA: Blackwell, 2005.

Alex F. McCalla and John Nash, eds. — *Reforming Agricultural Trade for Developing Countries.* Washington, DC: World Bank Publications, 2007.

Dragan Miljkovic, ed. — *Food Regulation and Trade.* Hauppauge, NY: Nova Science Publishers, 2007.

Arvind Panagariya — *India: The Emerging Giant.* New York: Oxford University Press, 2008.

Ralf Peters — *Roadblock to Reform: The Persistence of Agricultural Export Subsidies.* New York: United Nations Publications, 2006.

E. Wesley F. Peterson — *A Billion Dollars a Day: The Economics and Politics of Agricultural Subsidies.* Malden, MA: Wiley-Blackwell, 2009.

Sandra Polaski — *Winners and Losers: Impact of the Doha Development Round on Developing Countries*, Washington, DC: Carnegie Foundation, 2006.

Michael Pollan — *In Defense of Food: An Eater's Manifesto.* New York: Penguin, 2008.

Randy Schnepf and Jasper Womach — *Potential Challenges to U.S. Farm Subsidies in the WTO.* Hauppauge, NY: Nova Science Publishers, 2008.

Vandana Shiva — *Earth Democracy: Justice, Sustainability, and Peace.* Cambridge, MA: South End Press, 2005.

United Nations Conference on Trade and Development — *Roadblock to Reform: The Persistence of Agricultural Export Subsidies.* New York: United Nations Publications, 2006.

World Bank Publications — *World Development Report 2008: Agriculture and Development.* Washington, DC: World Bank Publications, 2007.

Julia Wright   *Sustainable Agriculture and Food Security in an Era of Oil Scarcity: Lessons from Cuba.* London: Earthscan Publications, 2008.

Nikolaos
Zahariadis   *State Subsidies in the Global Economy.* New York: Palgrave Macmillan, 2008.

Index

A